GO WITHIN
or
GO WITHOUT

A Simple Guide to
Self-Healing

GO WITHIN
or
GO WITHOUT

A Simple Guide to
Self-Healing

Gloria D. Benish

CITADEL PRESS
Kensington Publishing Corp.
http://www.kensingtonbooks.com

The information in this book is based solely on the experiences and information provided by the author. It is not intended to replace medical advice or treatment by your physician. Because every individual is unique, every reader will be subject to unique experiences. This book is meant to inspire and to evoke the self-healing capabilities of the individuals who read it.

CITADEL PRESS BOOKS are published by

Kensington Publishing Corp.
850 Third Avenue
New York, NY 10022

All Kensington Titles, Imprints, and Distributed Lines are available at special quantity discounts for bulk purchases for sales promotions, premiums, fund-raising, educational or institutional use. Special book excerpts or customized printings can also be created to fit specific needs. For details, write or phone the office of the Kensington special sales manager: Kensington Publishing Corp., 850 Third Avenue, New York, NY 10022, attn: Special Sales Department, Phone: 1-800-221-2647

Citadel Press and the Citadel logo are trademarks of Kensington Publishing Corp.

First Citadel Printing: September 2001
10 9 8 7 6 5 4 3 2 1

Printed in the United States of America

Library of Congress Control Number: 2001091782
ISBN 0-8065-2256-9

IN LOVING MEMORY

Of a single match, that became an eternal flame . . .

Cities, nor walls of flesh can keep us apart,

For we are forever one

To **God**, my partner,

To **Walter Zacharius**, for being the first publisher to ever realize "it wasn't just about publishing a book." For believing in the message and in me, and being willing to take the risk—I will be forever grateful! I'll never forget where it all began.

To my editor, **Claire Gerus**, who is capable of saying something in a single sentence or two, where it takes me pages and pages to get the same thought across. She is my hero, and if I'm ever able to develop her style of writing, I'll have to stop writing books and become a columnist instead.

Claire, as "my seeing-eye person," walked me through my initial trips to New York City, as well as the steps of the publishing industry. Until I saw how many times she sifted through every word of this manuscript, I was unaware of the duties of an editor. Her devotion to make this book the best it can be, is a gift to you and to me. I'm grateful to tell the world how much I appreciate her. If you enjoy this book, send her a silent blessing.

To **LuAnn Stallcop**, who ordained me as a Minister and Certified Spiritual Healer, so I could legally offer people *A Helping Hand*.

To **Susie Q. Leavines**, who inspired me with the title during coffee one day.

To my husband, **Kirk H. Benish,** my handsome knight in shining armor. The world wants a fairy tale, why not start with you and me? I give you my heart and soul, throughout eternity!

To my children, **Kerrie, Jaime, D.W., and Danielle**, who know me as Mom and don't mind sharing me with the world. (Not too much anyway.)

To my parents, **Esther and Allen Hale**, who I'm "not supposed to say mushy things about"—but I won't hesitate to tell the world that I love, honor, and respect them for all they taught me and for who they are.

To my dearest friend, **Linda K. Fudge**, who is just beginning to see her beauty, inside and out!

To **every friend** I've met along life's path, whether we had years or milliseconds together.

And to you, **the reader**—I hope, as you read this book, that you can *feel* the love that inspired me to write it. If you do, the book is a success.

CONTENTS

A Note to the Reader

Throughout this book, you will find references to Jesus, a Higher Power, the Holy Spirit, God, the divine, the creative force, and other terms for divinity. You may choose whichever of these you are comfortable with. Or you may substitute your own word. The bottom line is, we are each a spark of the divine—and this book will help you awaken the divine presence within you.

INTRODUCTION

If you as an adult don't have time to read this book, I ask you to pass it on to your child to read. Go *Within or Go Without* is written simply and very down-to-earth, and anyone above the age of eight will be able to understand it. Children are natural-born healers in my opinion, and I guess it's not really just an opinion because true experiences have led me to believe it.

Whenever children have turned to me to be healed, I have willingly done so. However, I also teach them how to do it themselves. The young and the young-at-heart need this information to use throughout the rest of their life. It was *my* child who taught me the principle, and I have used it every day of my life since. Teaching how is my service to each person I meet.

Children don't question why it works. It seems to be more of a reminder of something they already know. They don't need the words *God, spirit, principle, unconditional love,* or any of the other words to explain. Children accept the truth without question. In the Bible, we are asked "to become as little children." Need I say more?

When my daughter Danielle was eight years old, she asked me if she could buy a copy of my book *As God Is My Witness*. I laughed and said, "Danielle, you don't need to buy a copy. I'll just give you one." Then I asked, "Do you want me to autograph it for you?" She responded from her heart, "No . . . not really." (I had to laugh, because Danielle knew I wasn't really the author. The book wrote itself and God used it as a tool to heal fear, guilt, and judgment.)

Danielle read the introduction to *As God Is My Witness* aloud to me, stopping at times to sound out the words. She was reading it so haltingly that I was sure she wouldn't know what she read afterward. I was wrong.

As she finished, I asked, "Danielle, do you have any idea what you just read or what the introduction is saying?" She looked insulted as she replied, "Of course, Mom. It's saying that God didn't make the mess we're in on this planet, but if we're willing to help ourselves, He's willing to help us clean it up." I rest my case. (I also asked if she would join me as a motivational speaker in the days to come!)

Danielle is the child who taught me a decade ago to give others a little extra love, paving my way to be a spiritual healer. As you continue reading, you'll discover that everyone is special in ways we are all just now discovering.

I have so much love for you. I can't fake the love, the speeches before crowds, or the miracles that follow as a demonstration of that love. In case you didn't read the dedication of this book, I must repeat it: I hope, as you read this book, that you can feel the love that inspired me to write it. If you do, the book is a success. If you have already felt the love, then you don't need to read further. If you, however, want to feel more love each moment for the rest of your life, then I invite you to please continue to read.

I hope you're not too busy to drop everything and join me as I walk through a normal day in my life. I have one foot in the spiritual world and another in the physical world, remaining extremely well balanced, joyful, healthy, and content—while also having everything I need (usually before I know I need it). My desire is for each of you to say the exact same thing on a daily basis.

 **CHAPTER 1**

Sometimes the greatest
teachings can be taught
without saying a word—
Sometimes a smile says it all

My Dearest Friend,

I open my heart and home to you! Greetings and good morning from Montana, and welcome to my world! I awoke at 6:00 A.M. and before I ever got out of bed, I closed my eyes and placed my hands over them. Not only does this feel good while waking, allowing the warmth from my hands to soothe their coolness, but it opens my third eye so that I will have spiritual vision throughout the day.

I also rub my hands together and place them on the back of my head, near the base of the neck, which opens the seat to the soul, giving me a strong connection to the Light that will fill my physical being and guide my every step throughout the day.

Before I place my feet on the floor, I seek the Light within my soul to fill me with direction for that day. As a human, I may not be fully aware of what is truly important. The Light will go before me and prepare my way throughout the day.

After packing Kirk, my husband's, lunch and having a single cup of coffee with him, I walk him to the door and kiss him goodbye. I kneel on the couch and watch as he backs out of the driveway and, just before he pulls away, he throws me a kiss and I lip read his "I love you" as he drives away. My day begins with love on a spiritual level and becomes reality on a physical level.

I have four kids, but if you counted all those who call me Mom around town and in other cities, I'd probably be known as "the old woman who lived in a shoe and had so many children, she didn't know what to do."

I love kids. Kids love me. I'm a kid at heart.

I wear bells on my shoes and get pretty silly at times, though I'm in my forties. Last weekend, I telepathically heard a woman who was having a judgment about me and wishing I would act my age. In reality, I'm fourteen billion years old. Which age should I act?

I have one hour from the time Kirk leaves for work before I have to roust the kids to get them ready for school. Most days, I take that hour to open myself fully and completely to the Light. With my spiritual vision, I can see colors, and when I see the violet ray, I know that my life is in divine harmony and that the divine plan for that day of my life will unfold.

Today, as on all days, I awaken the children by singing "It's a beautiful day in the neighborhood" and they promise to get out of bed if I'll just stop singing. I prepare breakfast for them and then I unload the dishwasher, start laundry, make my bed and (yelling, if need be) remind each of them to make theirs. Being a spiritual mom doesn't mean you don't ever yell again!

Before they leave for school, I vacuum and spritz the living room, sweep the kitchen, and fly around the house at *mach* speed. In fact, a neighbor once asked me, "Where's your cape, Supermom?" "In the laundry," I replied with a grin.

My kids see to it that their rooms and the TV room are picked up, dirty socks thrown into the hamper, the dog and cat fed, and a load of wood hauled into the garage. (I figure that if they have time to fight, they have time and energy to work.)

It was my personal dream to be a mom. It was God's dream for me to be a spiritual healer and author. Fortunately, I'm able to do all three.

When the kids are gone, I just listen to the quiet. I sit in silence and ask God to fill my mind with what He thinks is important for me to do. Today, His Light filled my soul and mind with inspiration to write this book. The phone will ring constantly, people from all over the world asking for healings. I need to get groceries today, I am up to my eyeballs in dirty laundry, and I need to get ready to go out on promotion for four days at the end of this week, but I can trust God that writing a book won't interfere with all that I know is going on in my outer world.

There have been times when He's asked me to do things and I thought He'd lost His mind. Spirit appreciates us thinking for ourselves and using discernment, also. We're not to be mindless creatures, trusting foolishly.

In 1985, when God asked me to become a messenger and instructed me to "awaken millions and millions of His children from their past slumber of negative beliefs and fears, as well as healing the minds of mankind," I tried to pass up the job. After all, I had kids to raise. Didn't He realize what happened to messengers He sent into this realm?

Fears, at that time of my life, paralyzed me, and I had to be convinced that He was going to heal people through me without costing me too much human effort or I wasn't going to do it. I was quickly shown that it takes no human effort, so I really don't mind the job. (Actually, the position has pretty good benefits.)

Before I get started yak-attacking, I need to call our daughter Kerrie at United Space Alliance. Kerrie figures the jet propulsion for shuttle missions. (If you think I'm far out, you ought to meet her!) I also need to let Jaime, our twenty-two-year-old, know that I'll baby-sit my grandson, Colton, tomorrow night.

People think when they become spiritual that they need to quit their jobs so they can perform their Service to God. That doesn't make any sense to me. You don't quit your livelihood so you can be spiritual—you incorporate spirituality into every single day, doing whatever it is that you're already doing.

Being spiritual doesn't mean that you become a hermit. It means that you carry that knowingness, love, and principle so that all the people you meet throughout your entire day will be touched by your Light.

Since I am a third-generation motormouth, this will be hard for you to believe, but I don't have to talk about it, because I live it. Sometimes the greatest teachings can be taught without saying a word. Sometimes a smile says it all.

CHAPTER 2

Before they call, I will answer

My life is an open book! When I married my knight in shining armor four years ago, I forewarned him, "Be careful what you say or do because it might end up in print." Kirk laughed and replied, "Okay, but just don't write about our sex life." (He didn't tell me I couldn't talk about it, though.)

I have a healing state of consciousness, but the point is not for me to heal you or I would spend an entire life healing the world—today a broken arm, tomorrow a broken heart. What is important is for me to teach *you* how to heal your life, to give you the awareness so that you can put it to use throughout every single moment for the rest of your life. That's my service to God and to you.

I am being invited to cities to teach healing workshops that run from 9:00 A.M. to 6:00 P.M., with a one-hour break. Believe it or not, this full day hardly affords me the time to teach you all you need to know. Not that it's difficult, because in three lines I could teach anyone "how to do it." Eight hours is the time I need to tell you how it all began, why it happens, and how miracles can occur for you.

In the amount of time it would take for me to be present and teach you, I can put the same words on paper so you will have a physical reminder just in case senility sets in on you early, as it does for me at times.

For this moment in time, I want you to feel as if you are sitting at my dining room table, one on one, receiving nurturing, knowledge, a piece of my homemade apple pie, and maybe even dinner if you end up staying that long.

I love to feed people. It doesn't matter if it's physically or spiritually. I love to cook, but I also love to see people enjoying it.

I put all of myself into everything I do, whether it's mopping my kitchen floor, standing before hundreds of people, or giving healing hugs after an inspirational talk. I love my life! I want you to be able to say the same.

My bread is rising and while I'm dicing vegetables for a beef stew for tonight's meal, I want to begin by telling you some of my past. It's important for you to realize that I wasn't a spiritual seeker when all of the mystical experiences began in 1985. I was a normal, common housewife and mother, basically minding my own business.

I wasn't highly religious in the sense of going to church. I had been baptized and confirmed Presbyterian, but walked away from religion when I was fourteen years old. To me, life itself is a religious celebration. I am Christian in the sense of being kind, caring, sharing, and loving. To all religions, as well as the *New Age*, I am neutral. I belong to no religious denomination, cult, or group of people. I belong to God.

Like all of you, I was living life the hard, human way. I was married for nineteen years to a man who was periodically laid off from work, leaving us wondering where his next job would lead us. My past was spent in fear of getting sick. We sometimes had no insurance benefits. We couldn't afford to get sick. It seemed that it was feast or famine. Either we had extra money and we used it to gratify our human senses, or we were struggling fearfully on meager savings. Until I became spiritual, I never lived with peace of mind.

This all changed ten years into my first marriage. I couldn't get pregnant and I was very frustrated. "Why can't I have children like everyone else?" I asked my husband over and over again. Finally, because I wanted to have children so badly, I endured a series of costly—and often humiliating—tests to determine what was wrong.

I found out that endometriosis had bent my uterus backward and cemented it to my bowels. No wonder I couldn't get pregnant! "You'll have to have surgery," the doctors told me. "It's your only hope." So I booked a date with my surgeon and went into the hospital. The doctor successfully cut the endometriosis free and stitched my uterus in the correct position. After a short recovery time, I was told, I could try to get pregnant. But six weeks after the surgery, I pushed on a restaurant door and felt the stitches snap loose. Back to the doctor I went. After looking me over, he gave me two choices: to have a second operation or to stand on my head after making love, so the uterus would fall into the correct position. One operation is enough, I told myself. I'll try standing on my head. But that didn't work, either. I decided that, if I was meant to be a mother, it would happen someday; I decided to just "let go."

Another year passed. One day, I was with a group of small children when I felt the yearning rise within me again. And so, I decided to pray. I really didn't know the "right" way, so I just closed my eyes and asked silently, "God, why can't I have kids?" Behind my closed eyelids, I saw a long, dark tunnel. Within it, a white light was traveling toward me. It got larger and larger, and then, out of the light, walked Jesus. This may sound strange, but I wasn't surprised. I felt very calm and matter-of-fact, and when He approached, I asked, "How come I can't have kids?" He smiled, and replied, "I have three to give you. Please be patient." Then, He bent over to hug me, kissed my cheek, and turned to walk away. Three months later, I was pregnant.

Until I spiritually awakened at age thirty-two, I didn't even know what the word "spiritual" meant. I had been overprotected my entire life; I didn't know what a lot of things meant. To some degree, I'm still innocent of many things that you and others may live with on a daily basis.

Recently a woman come to me, telling me she had MS. Fortunately, I was able to say, "I don't know what MS does. I know that it stands for multiple sclerosis, but that's all I know about it. I have no idea what the symptoms or causes are." The woman started to tell me and I interrupted to say that I didn't need to know and that it was probably better if I didn't. If my human personality heard the explanation, I might get frightened or overwhelmed, believing it couldn't be healed. There is no order of difficulty in miracle working, but I'm not effective if I'm scared, nor are you.

I worked on the woman three times, for approximately thirty minutes each session. She returned to Denver and made a visit to her doctor. She authoritatively told him, "My MS is healed. I want you to take the appropriate tests and validate me." He performed the tests and his response to her was, "Your MS is healed." (She never did tell him she had come to see me.)

My point in sharing this particular story is this: You are not effective if you're frightened because fear creates a power in opposition to God (a God of love, one power, one presence, one experience). I do not promote fear. I heal it by dissolving it in the Light which flows through me. When fear no longer exists, perfection and healing manifest the true self.

Cancer, multiple sclerosis, AIDS, and all the varieties of diseases and pains are just words, nothing more. Man does not have the power to create a disease. Humankind only has the power to create a belief in a disease. Once the belief is purified, through the Light, within a consciousness, it disappears.

This sounds a bit confusing, I'm sure. Let's have a cup of hot spiced tea and I'll share more of what led up to this point of my teaching. I'll fold the clothes in the dryer and put another load in the washer during this time-out. If you like homemade chocolate-chip cookies, you can help yourself to some from the canister on the counter.

Years ago, when Danielle was nearly three years old, I was lying down one day with a headache. She came into my bedroom and asked, "Why are you lying down, Mom?" I responded, "I have a headache, Danielle, but I'm okay. I'll be up in a few minutes."

Immediately, she said, "Oh, you just need a little extra love." She rubbed her two little hands together and placed one of them on my navel and the other on my breastbone. She closed her eyes and tilted her head back. Confused as to what she was doing, I questioned, "Danielle, what do you see?"

She responded, "I see red, orange, yellow, green, blue, and purple." She then gasped as she said, "Oh, Mom! I just saw White Light! I just saw God!" My eyes widened in disbelief and I asked, "You saw God?" She smiled and said, "Oh, yes, and He loves us so very much!"

My headache disappeared and I was in total confusion. First of all, we never talked about God in our home (okay, unless we were using His name in vain). Danielle had never been taught anything about God. Nor had she learned the colors of the spectrum, not even from *Sesame Street!* Something had occurred, something beyond her sharing "a little extra love."

Weeks later, I was visiting my parents in Denver. My mom continued to complain about a painful elbow. Being almost sarcastic, I decided to imitate Danielle by saying to my mother, "Oh, you just need a little extra love." I rubbed my two hands together as Danielle had. I placed them on my mom's elbow, closed my eyes, and tilted my head back.

I didn't see colors as Danielle had. Instead, I saw my mother slip on the ice at Lowry Air Force Base (where she worked) and when she came down, she hit her tailbone and cracked her elbow. Until that moment, I didn't know I was clairvoyant. I told my mother what I'd seen and she affirmed that, indeed, it had happened just as I'd envisioned. "In fact," she said, "it happened a year ago and my elbow has hurt ever since." She surprised me by saying, "But, son of a b . . . it doesn't hurt anymore!" I responded brilliantly with, "You're kidding?"

Upon returning home from Denver, I received a call at noon from a friend named Rosemary. Her first words to me were, "I want to come to you for a healing." I literally laughed aloud and questioned, "What makes you think I can do anything?" With deep trust and sincerity in her voice, she explained that the month before, she had been lying on her back in bed, in severe pain. She couldn't get out of bed because she hurt so badly. She said, "After just talking to you on the phone, I was able to get out of bed, pain free."

I said, "Rosemary, I don't know what I did then, so I don't know what I can do now." She seemed to have faith in me, but I was skeptical. I asked her to share her experience, but concluded that I could probably only offer her a kind word or an affirmation.

She began telling me that she had been bleeding severely for a long time. The doctors had done a D&C, but she hadn't stopped bleeding and now they wanted to do a complete hysterectomy, which she didn't want.

I could hear her words, but something was making my eyes so heavy that I couldn't keep them open. I quit resisting whatever was occurring within my inner vision. I could see a beautiful violet light flooding into the center of my vision from the left and right. When it got to the center point, it flowed outward with great force. I could hear what she was saying, but I was completely mesmerized by this beautiful light.

When she finished talking, I could once again open my eyes. I said, "Rosemary, it's Friday at noon. Why don't you come see me Monday, at noon? I don't know what I can do, but just come."

Over the weekend, I forgot all about the incident. So on Monday when the doorbell rang, I was embarrassed when I saw Rosemary standing there. I invited her in, trying to cover up my embarrassment. I said, "Rosemary, I'm sorry, I forget why you're here." She questioned, "Don't you remember, I was bleeding?" Relieved, I answered, "Oh, that's right." Continuing, she asked, "But, did you do something already? Because I haven't bled since we talked on the phone Friday." With charm and humility, and total truthfulness, I said, "Yes, but I don't know what I did."

For the following three years, I continued to respond just as brilliantly. Every time a miracle occurred through me, I always sealed it with, "You're kidding?" Word spread like wildfire. Gloria can do this, but Gloria didn't know what she was doing.

People would phone me and, as soon as they heard my voice, they were healed. I would taste and smell purity as people were healed through me. One day, in between telephone calls, I questioned aloud, "God, what on earth is happening in my world?" A silent, inner voice boldly said, "Before they call, I will answer!"

I turned to ministers, but they didn't know what to do with me.

I scared most of them, I'm sure. One woman called me an angel of Satan, which devastated me. I knew my powers had nothing to do with Satan, because I could see my personal guide, the Source, and He would telepathically tell me what to do.

Yes, I was gifted with not only clairvoyance and clairaudience, but also telepathy, healing, and many, many other gifts. I had no conscious knowledge about these gifts until I began reading books. I could just do it. In fact, I could do it easily—and so can you.

Some people, most in fact, tested me on a daily basis. "Show me a miracle and I'll believe. . . ." Well, I showed them! I showed them, not by having to do anything, but just by loving them, which, for the most part, is an unconscious effort.

Some of the tests were funny from my point of view. A man who was testing my telepathy found out the hard way that I could hear the thoughts and judgments of others. I had spent an hour sitting with him at my dining room table. My two toddlers were arguing and I headed down the hall to quiet them. I stopped in mid-stride, turned to him, and responded, "Thank you." He questioned, "For what?" I answered truthfully, "Well, you thought I had a cute little walk and a nice little ass." Embarrassed, he asked, "You know that?" Red faced, I said, "I know that and more." He tested me further and after I validated his thoughts, his face and mine matched.

Let's take another time-out as you think of any questions you might want to ask. My husband, Kirk, has told me that I overwhelm people. I don't mean to. Miracles and experiences such as these are so everyday and so normal to me that I really don't think of them as miracles at all anymore. Let me give you a little time to assimilate this information and then we'll continue. I have so much to say if someone will just listen to me. How about another cup of tea?

CHAPTER 3

*I hold out my hands to you,
not to take from you
through greed,
but to offer you loving support*

I have a few minutes before I have to fold another load of laundry, so I think we should break for lunch before I tell you about more miracles. I hope you like crab. I take the imitation crab, dice some celery into it, a tidbit of diced green onion, a tablespoon of lemon juice, mix a little mayonnaise into it, and spread it atop a toasted bagel. I hope you like tomato because I like to set it on the crab, open-faced. Mmmm, mmmm, once again, made with loving hands. Would you like a slice of cantaloupe and a few blueberries on the side just for color? Being a Libra, I really like to have my food served pretty. There's plenty for everyone, so enjoy!

So many metaphysicians and those on the spiritual path believe that they have to give up certain things as they achieve a heightened sense of awareness. I never gave up meat or even my Diet Dr. Peppers! I only gave up a belief that there was a power beyond that of God that could harm my body. Chocolates, sugar, meat, or any of those physical things may gradually fall away as the human judgment is healed, but nothing of a physical nature has to be denied to live a spiritual life.

The world seems to be motivated by greed, the belief that there isn't enough, and that if I have something, you can't. That's a false belief. Everything, and I mean everything, is born of consciousness. Consciousness is that which already exists without taking form as human thought, which, in spiritual reality, is what your true essence is. This means that no human mental process is needed to maintain your life. With my inner vision, pure consciousness appears as liquid Light, and with my outer vision, it looks like a blizzard of snowflakes. Consciousness is universal God substance. It *is* God, everywhere present, all powerful, divine intelligence.

Consciousness manifests as the food I eat, the clothing I wear, the home I live in, the love I experience through people, gifts, or the car I drive. Consciousness unfolds, through my individual mind, as everything I will ever need in this life.

People don't need money. People need to open their minds to allow that unlimited energy source/stream of consciousness to fill their minds with the divine plan and perfection that is their birthright.

Seekers don't need to sacrifice anything in order to heighten their awareness of this power. God/love/consciousness/Light doesn't ask us to do anything to receive the unconditional love.

Metaphysicians speak poetically about unconditional love, but they fail to recognize that the love must pass through an *unconditioned mind*. The Master was who He was because He had surrendered every human judgment. He had attained a totally unconditioned mind, which allowed Him to maintain His inner peace regardless of the outer appearance.

One evening when He came to me, He said, "If you truly believe that I performed those acts as stated in ancient writings, don't idolize Me . . . raise your conscious awareness and *just do it.*" I incorporated that philosophy into my everyday world. If I receive an idea, I don't sit around thinking about it, I just do it! You see, I had spent an entire life in procrastination and fear. (In the amount of time it takes you to think about it, you could just do it.) A second philosophy of mine became, Feel the fear and do it anyway.

In mid-November, I was invited to the Pacific Northwest to perform individual healings for three days. On the third day, just before lunch, I was healing a woman and, while doing so, I saw Him with my spiritual vision. He was standing before me, cloaked

in a white ceremonial robe sewn with golden threads. He telepathically asked me to join Him later in a ceremony of mastery. I said
nothing aloud to the woman I was healing. I just continued to
watch the inner healing Light.

When we finished with a heart-to-heart hug, she asked, "Did
you also see Jesus standing before us?" Surprised, I replied, "Yes." I
also shared the message, not knowing whether it was for the
woman, or me, or both of us. We made a pact to stay in touch and
share whatever occurred later that day or evening.

We said our good-byes and my companion, June Nelson, and I
left for lunch, needing to return by one o'clock to resume with
more individuals. When we arrived at the restaurant, it was
crowded with people coming from Sunday services. I asked the
hostess of the restaurant for a table for two and was told that it
would be at least a twenty-minute wait.

My attention was drawn to a table (for two) near the kitchen
area, but I said nothing. Immediately, the hostess turned her head
and saw the same table, responding, "Oh, I do have a table for two.
It will be just a moment before I can seat you."

June and I were seated and our orders taken immediately. We
discussed the morning's healings and I looked around the restaurant, noticing several people that I would have liked to get my
hands on.

Our food arrived quickly and, though normally I'm a slow eater,
this day I found myself finishing quickly. When I looked at my
watch, it was 12:45 P.M. June and I had fifteen minutes before we
had to be back at the home to meet with people who had appoint-
ments.

June, however, had not even bitten into her cheeseburger.
Rather than feeling fear or stress, I said, "June, take your time and
enjoy your meal. I'm sure we will be back on time, but I have to go
to the car. I don't know why, but I just have to go."

I was feeling rather embarrassed and thinking myself rude. I had
never, in my entire life, excused myself and left a friend sitting
alone in a restaurant. Nevertheless, I had to go.

I sat in the car and was only there for milliseconds when I felt
like I was being called. My attention was pulling me to literally

turn completely around to look toward the front of the restaurant and when I did, I saw an older man bent over in pain.

This stranger had gotten as far as the newspaper stand outside the restaurant and had stopped, bending over and placing his head on his right hand.

My thoughts whispered, Go to him. I immediately felt fear. How could I approach a total stranger and tell him that I'm a healer? How could anyone be so bold? I just couldn't do it.

My thoughts became urgent and repeated, Go to him *now*! I breathed a heavy sigh and, as I was reaching for the car door handle, I was silently asking God to give me the strength and courage to do this.

Walking across the parking lot and approaching the stranger, I began my introduction, "Sir, my name is Gloria Benish. Please be patient with me because I've never done anything like this before in my life. I'm an ordained minister and a spiritual healer. Would you mind very much if I laid hands on your lungs?"

Without raising his head, he gave me permission. In broad daylight, standing outside a restaurant, in full view of all those sitting inside the restaurant, I rubbed my hands together, laid them on his back at the lung area, and closed my eyes asking for God's peace and grace to flow through me.

Beneath my hands, it felt as though there was a raging, burning forest fire. I felt so much pain from him that I could only take deep breaths and exhale. I wanted to cry from the pain that this man carried. I literally feel the pain of another, but, if I can feel it, I can heal it.

His wife approached us, asking what was going on. Without opening my eyes, I explained briefly who I was, what I was attempting to do, and that her husband had given permission. I heard her silent judgment that I was doing this for a monetary reward, and I replied, "I don't charge. I do what I do because I love people so very much." I opened my eyes just long enough to look into her eyes following my reply.

I saw the healing Light within the man's left lung and could feel the heat dissolving. I felt a coolness under my palm and I knew that the left lung was healed.

June came out of the restaurant at this time and I heard her teasingly say, "I can't leave you alone for a moment." Her comment seemed to help the wife. I understood the skepticism of the woman. It's not every day that a stranger would assist out of kindness or that a "miracle worker" would approach someone in pain in public.

The right lung was still blazing hot beneath my touch and I felt human fear enter that I wouldn't have enough time to complete the healing. My concerns became my reality as I heard his wife say, "The car is here for us. We have to leave now."

At this same time, the man began to crumple to the concrete. I held him with all my strength and supported his entire weight. To an onlooker, that would have appeared a miracle in itself. I'm four foot eleven and weigh about one hundred pounds. To support this gentleman's weight, I knew that I must have had an army of angels helping me.

I was moving him toward the vehicle and June offered to help get him to the car. Once at the open door, he sat, with me still supporting him to get his legs inside. Fully seated, he turned to look at me and our eyes met for the first time. With complete sincerity, he said, "Thank you so very much." Tears sprang to my eyes.

As I was pulling my left arm out from where it rested between the man's back and the car seat, my left hand brushed across that right lung. As it did, I saw the Light, the heat dissolved, and I believe the lung was healed.

Tears then burst forth and I embraced the wife. Through my crying I was saying, "I think I healed it! I think I got it! Oh, my God, he was hurting so badly, but I think I got it!" As we released from the hug, she moved her left hand toward me and opened it, offering cash.

I couldn't believe it! I'm sure I didn't handle it well. An unexpected sharp tone filled my voice as I said, "I didn't do it for money!" Surprised, she questioned, "You mean you really don't want the money?" I replied, "No. I told you that I do what I do because I love people so much." She got into the backseat of the vehicle, still dazed, I'm sure, by all that had occurred in the last fifteen minutes.

As for me, I was sobbing. June asked me if I wanted a hug, but I just wanted to get into my car and cry. First of all, I had never openly admitted to anyone publicly that I could do what I do. I had done all of my service privately until two months earlier when I was invited to Spokane, Washington, to teach a healing workshop. Previously, I had only been heard of through word-of-mouth or through a friend or family member. This day at the restaurant was my coming-out party.

I was also embarrassed to cry in public. I tried never to cry in front of people because I cry so ugly. I had felt two of my fears and did it anyway.

Once in the car, I rested my elbows on the steering wheel and placed my hands over my eyes and bawled like a baby. As I remember, my words to June were something like this, "I had to do it. Oh, God, I had to do it, that man was hurting so bad!"

I didn't have much time to process what had just happened because I was due back at the home to continue healings for the remainder of the afternoon. On the way back to "work," I told June, "My thoughts say, If I walk with divine love, what is there to fear? If divine love, itself, had been sitting in the car and had felt another's pain, would it have hesitated, wondering if it would be rejected or fearing that it might get sued? I don't think so. Would He ever hesitate for a moment to reach out and help anyone? I don't think so. Then if I'm going to be used as an instrument to heal and follow in His footsteps, I don't think I'd better hesitate ever again."

Just before lunch, He had said that He would join me later in a ceremony of Mastery. I certainly hadn't imagined that He had meant so soon.

I may never hear whether the man's lungs were healed, but I did what I could in that moment in time. How many miracles can you count in this one experience? My kindnesses and all miracles are generated from the love within myself.

Society promotes fear of reaching out to others or getting involved. That teaching is a part of my past. I'm not saying that I will never again feel any resistance to reaching out, but I will totally trust and take action as much as possible.

I had been afraid of rejection—like all of us. My love has been rejected in personal relationships and I didn't want to open myself to ridicule or rejection from a stranger. Fifteen years ago, when my spiritual experiences and the miracles began occurring and He asked me to write a book that would awaken millions and millions of His children from their negative beliefs and fears, as well as heal the minds of mankind, I thought He had made the wrong choice in asking me.

I was the world's largest "chicken McNugget," scared of every-one and everything. He insisted that, for this reason alone, I'd be the perfect person for the job. For the past decade, I've been healing every fear that presents itself within me. What I teach, be-lieve, and do, does work! The messages I share, personally or through my books, aren't mine: They're spirit's messages. I'm just the messenger.

To complete this story, two weeks after I had this experience, while in a mall doing my Christmas shopping, I heard a woman asking, "Is that Gloria Benish?" I turned to see the woman whom I had healed before lunch that day and who also had seen Him. We were able to share the completion of that experience, fulfilling our verbal pact. She, also, had had a mystical experience.

You see, my protection (or yours) doesn't come from paper and ink, a ministry, or anything in this physical world. Your protection is your consciousness of God, and through the outpouring of that spirit, you'll know your true inner security.

During my spiritual growth years ago, my Teacher also said, "Because you have such a strong desire to know how it was that I walked on water, tonight it is My great pleasure to teach you." We transcended time and space and were standing on the ocean shore. He said, "I never looked to man, nor earth to sustain Me. I looked only to infinite spirit's love."

I teach others, because of this, to have a total dependency upon God alone, not to look without, to me or to others, but to seek within. This is why I don't encourage people to come to me on a continual basis; however, I will always be there for those in need. On the first visit, I nurture them, as well as bring forth the healing consciousness. By the second visit, they feel more comfortable with me and are discovering confidence within themselves. On the third visit, I teach them all I know and send them on their way.

With that teaching came the understanding of why I could never charge anyone for performing healings. I don't depend upon a paycheck or on "sick people" to provide for me. I am not attempting to live like a queen, at another's expense. By placing my attention upon my true source of supply, my conscious awareness of God—I open my mind for that which already exists to flow from within to the without. Simply stated, I will not place my attention upon physical things that appear as supply, but you can bet your bippy that I wouldn't go a day without allowing that violet Light to flood into my awareness. By flooding my awareness with the Light, the supply then may appear to come in the form of a paycheck, a donation, a gift or a bag of carrots or potatoes in exchange for a healing. However, in not looking to the outer effects first, but seeking the Light within, all else will appear.

I admit that at first I didn't quite understand why I couldn't charge. It was an inner knowingness that unfolded from the following experience. In the first two weeks of realizing the healing talent within me, I flew to Arizona to visit family. I was there for two weeks, sharing my talents with family and strangers. I was dealing with many poverty-level people. Though I was only charging a quarter, one woman said to me, "I don't even have a quarter to give." I hugged her and replied, "I'll just put yours on account!" She smiled and asked, "You mean, when I get a quarter, I can send it to you?" I smiled in return and said, "No, on account of I love you!"

When I returned home, I removed the quarters from a small pouch. I counted fifty-two and silently said to myself, "Fifty-two quarters! Look how many people I helped!" It felt as though I had been kicked in the stomach as an inner unvoiced message followed, "I helped no one. God helped fifty-two people *through me*." I never charged again.

Friends thought I was setting myself up as superior by not charging. Hardly. I knew that I was doing nothing. By myself, I could not even cure a headache, unless I asked someone to take two

Tylenol and call me in the morning. A power greater than myself was performing the works. As the years of growing evolved and the Higher Power worked through me, the teachings from within began to unfold into my outer world.

As humans, we only need to open our individual mind for the presence of God/the creative force/the Holy Spirit/the Higher Power (choose one) that is within to flow into the outer world of form. In this or any other situation, it's all we can do.

I hold out my hands to you, not to take from you through greed, but to offer you loving support. Think on these things, find and yield to the peace within, and the without will always take care of itself.

CHAPTER 4

I am a witness for God—
I promise to tell the truth,
the whole truth,
and nothing but the truth!

I could never understand why it was so difficult to become published when God Himself had asked me to write the books, which He actually wrote through me. I questioned Him. After all, when He gave Noah the idea, He also gave him the dimensions with which to build the Ark. Now, I knew how Noah felt!

It wasn't until recently that I learned that I needed to grow to the level of consciousness that could manifest outwardly as publisher, financial backing, distributor, speaking engagements, and the healings. You will soon understand this idea more as you continue reading.

Within the spiritual idea to write was the energy and the fulfillment of that request. I have been within the spiritual world and have witnessed the reality of every soul I have met or will ever meet. It's not about *becoming*; it's about *being*.

I recently was the instrument through which a woman was to be healed. I could feel her pain, so deeply embedded within her body that I felt I would not be able to dissolve it fast enough. I was consumed with the feeling of rage that came from her. I asked her to place the person she hated most in her mind. She refused, saying, "I can't."

I explained that the Light was present, so the hate would not leave the room and hurt the person nor would it hurt her any longer. She questioned, "But, what if it's God that I hate? I can't hate God!" I held this woman in my arms and whispered, "Oh, yes, you can."

The rage and hate came up and out of her in violent gags and vomiting. She sobbed and I sobbed with her. Uncontrollable tears flowed down our faces. When she finished, I continued to hold her in my arms, knowing that it wasn't God she hated, but the falsely taught concept of God. There's a big difference.

In coming to me, she hadn't requested a physical healing. Rather, she had requested a mystical experience, wanting to feel the presence of God and her oneness with that power. Following the healing, I sat behind her, caressing her face and wiping away her tears. I asked, "Do you feel that warmth coming from my heart?" She nodded her head, "Yes." I said, "That's God. Not the concept you've been taught, but what God truly is."

I questioned her a second time. "I felt your pain, didn't I?" She again nodded her head, "Yes." I questioned a third time, "And I cried your tears, didn't I?" She nodded once again. I said, "Well, I've felt your pain, but I've also felt your love, so I guess you could say you received your mystical experience of feeling oneness." We nearly collapsed from the knowingness and love present.

This brings me to explain how and why *As God Is My Witness* was written. I live in the Bitterroot Valley, surrounded by the Rocky Mountains. From my office window, I can see a peak of the Rockies, named St. Mary's. The town where I live is the oldest community in Montana. According to folklore, back in the 1800s, a dying Indian child received a visit from Mother Mary. The mountain and the legend inspire me.

One morning, as I was sitting behind my office desk, looking out at the Big Sky and the peak, I began to see a movie unfold with my eyes open. I began writing down what I was seeing and, within eighteen hours, the manuscript had not only been handwritten, but was also typed into the computer. (I actually had to write the epilogue first, just to get it out of my head.)

I sent the manuscript to a Virginia-based publisher, who read and enjoyed it. He telephoned me, stating that he was regrettably going to have to return it because the publishing house was overextended financially for that spring. Just before he hung up, he said, "Gloria, this doesn't happen very often, but this book does not even need to be edited."

While the book was on its way back to me in Montana, I told Kirk that there were a couple places in the book I wasn't comfortable with and that when I got it back, I was going to cut those places and add to it to make it a bigger book. That night, I had a dream and a bold inner voice said, "Do not edit one word."

I was also guided to create Miracle Publishing Company and, even in the dream, I was arguing, "I didn't know how to be a publisher. I don't have the money to be a publisher . . ." The voice said, "Be at peace."

I went to print with *As God Is My Witness* so quickly, I didn't know what hit me. However, I couldn't promote it. I tried and was met with adversity. I backed off and could do nothing with the book. Two years passed before I could confidently stand in its defense, through nonresistance, which is synonymous with the peace that passeth all human understanding, the key to healing every aspect of your life.

Witness is written in four parts. God is on trial for seven crimes against humanity and He has asked me to be His defender, demonstrating and proving His innocence. I have seven days to go into the prison and prepare His defense. As the trial begins, I'm overwhelmed. In the "Testimony," He takes the stand and speaks in First Person. And then there's the verdict.

I understood so much through writing that book. Even when my Teacher walked the Earth, He never got a trial to demonstrate His innocence. And, how many of us, in today's society, could actually raise our hands and swear on a Bible that we know God? Not some concept of God that we've been taught by others or through writings, but an actual experience of *knowing* God? God is an experience, not an intellectual concept.

Experience of God brings hope to a tired world. Personally, whenever I feel overwhelmed by the sense that I'm "not doing enough," I open the pages of that book, at random, and find comfort.

This book is unfolding the same way. Before I began this morning, I opened my mind to the consciousness of God, knowing that this book has already been written. I am an instrument, being used by God and, by God, I promise to tell the truth, the whole truth, and nothing but the truth (so help me, God!)

CHAPTER 5

When you can look upon any situation,
with a peaceful state of mind,
the judgment will be healed

Now that we've had lunch, would you please join me on a walk through our neighborhood so I can walk our Sheltie, Roco. He looks forward to these walks and it will give us a chance to get some fresh air and physical exercise. It gives me a minute away from the interruptions of the telephone as well.

Each day at noon, except on this day, of course, I go within to reach out to that heightened sense of awareness, so that I stand ready when people call on me. I attempt to stay at that level of consciousness throughout each day, or I'm not effective for others or myself. Rest assured, I *am* at that state of healing consciousness.

My family and I live simply, in a normal neighborhood. I know most of the neighbors personally and I appreciate each and every one of them. We're a middle-class-income family. Kirk is an instrument technician at a paper mill about an hour away from our home. I have never worked outside the home since I had children. I haven't had much time to do so.

I remember back about seven years ago, I was feeling I needed a paycheck to contribute something to the family income. I meditated and contemplated, and then became confused because I wasn't really sure how I was going to have a job and do everything else that I do as well. One morning, in the quiet, God responded, "If I truly thought that you would be fulfilled working outside the home, I would prepare a place for you within society. However, you are performing the divine plan of your life. Be at peace."

God is always telling me to be at peace. It wasn't until dogs began tearing into our trash every Monday morning that I found the mystical meaning behind those words. I had dreaded Monday mornings because I would have to go out and pick up the trash from the street, and I hated to get my hands dirty. I know that we attract what we love, hate, and fear, but I really hated it.

I would look at all the other homes surrounding us and no one else's trash was in the street. So, like so many of us, I would silently scream, Why me? I meditated and the message for me was this: The dogs tear into your trash because you have a judgment that it's bad. When you can look upon this or any situation, with a neutral/peaceful state of mind, the judgment will be healed.

My inner voice followed with, If those dogs want to come every Monday morning and tear up my trash, that's okay. If not, that's okay, too. Peace be with me. I felt an inner shift and the dogs never returned. (Shift happens . . . !)

I then incorporated this teaching into every aspect of my life. The moment I stopped believing that it was good if I had money and bad if I didn't, I healed the judgment in my mind. Within our own mind is the only place we can begin.

When I (re)discovered the truth of this simple teaching, I could look upon every situation, every day, and remove all judgment of good and bad. We're taught, from youth, that there are opposing forces: Satan and God. As a small child, I never believed there was a Satan. Something inside me just told me that.

If we believe in opposing forces, the judgments of the world will consume us, not because we deserve it, but, because we are part of a collective or group consciousness. We don't consciously hold thoughts to bring disease to us, but if we believe in two powers, this is our experience. Thought, of itself, except under karmic or mental law, has no power. Karmic law is a mesmerizing suggestion, induced into mass consciousness. In ultimate/spiritual reality, there is only one power, one presence, and one experience. Everything else is a by-product of illusion under karmic law, and must be healed individually.

Let's return to my home so I can share more information and miracles with you. By the end of this day, I trust you will understand that all miracles are born of love. One truly isn't more difficult than another. Like dreams becoming reality, they are ultimate expressions of love.

CHAPTER 6

Because I seek no glory,
payment,
or even a thank you,
I'm able to heal those I walk amongst

Several people called while we were out, but because they didn't get to talk to me doesn't mean that they don't receive their healing. Let me explain. The moment a person reaches out to my consciousness (or the higher consciousness of another individual), the healing is received in that moment. Remember when Jesus was surrounded by the masses and a woman reached out to touch his robe and received healing? It could be symbolic or literal. My "robe" is my consciousness and when people think of me, and of that identity that is the divine within me, they receive their miracles.

The reason that I may have to go into the Light more than once for a person is because the belief/condition/nature of error has been deeply imbedded within consciousness. My motto is, I'll keep doing it until I get it right. By the way, I'm not a faith healer. In the beginning, I was skeptical and people still received their miracles. Those who have no faith have also received healings, so the miracles are not dependent upon faith. The source is within everyone, whether they are consciously aware or accepting of it or not.

The simple truth is that I have to make a strong connection to "the source." Once that occurs, a person is healed. If that fails to occur, I need to heighten *my* consciousness, not theirs, and in that process, I am usually electrified and the shift in the physical world occurs.

Concerning the electric shock, it hurts in a good way. It's like plugging 110-volt human power into 220-volt supreme power. These have literally lifted me off the bed or couch. I also call the electrifying a "shift," which is indicative of a "shift in perception" that shifts the consciousness from human to divine, and dis-ease (illusion) to health (spiritual reality).

I have healing hands, which means that I am able to transfer unconditional/ unlimited/universal energy to a person. The body *can* heal itself, but it needs energy to do so. Remember Rosemary? Hers was an absentee healing. I was able to heal with my mind over a great distance. Since I am working with the consciousness of God, a physical body does not limit me when reaching out to others. I am where my consciousness is.

I can transfer the energy through my hands or use my mind over long distances. Don't let those words confuse you, because healing over long distances is not a mental-imaging healing. I take no thought, name, or "disease" into the Light. I call forth the Light from within my individual consciousness and allow that Light to dissolve the darkness (error/fear/pain.) Once my individual mind is purified of human judgment or belief, the person, no matter where he or she is on the globe, receives healing.

I do not need my hands as tools to heal. Nor do you. However, I will teach you how to use your hands for healing, because many people respond more readily to something physical. (I call it being "user-friendly.")

Because I seek no glory, payment, or even a thank you, I am able to heal those I walk among. Many throughout the last ten years, have been totally unaware of the source of their healings. Recognition or reward are not important, to me, for I am healing my own consciousness (of error) at the same time!

Now do you understand why I don't charge a fee? Since you and I are one in the mind of God I'm healing an aspect of myself. I'm not just being poetic or a phyzz head when I say we are one. It is truth. (By the way, a phyzz head is someone who has absorbed metaphysical theories, beyond useful application, and has lost balance with this dimension and purpose. It may sound as though I'm in judgment, but there is a fine line between judgment and discernment.)

You also can do what I do. I have had people ask me, How do we know that you're not special or chosen by God to do this, and that we're not? Trust me! I'm only chosen by God to teach you this information and the only time I'm "special," is when I want to have my way with Kirk.

Everyone can do this. A recent experience will show how easy it is to do. You don't have to chant, smudge yourself, or create an elaborate ceremony (unless you choose to do so).

The following occurred while I was in Denver this past summer, promoting my books and doing healings. I was staying with my sister, Sheila. I had left my son D.W. and Danielle with my sister's two girls and had gone out that morning to do healings. I returned home around noon and found eight kids screaming in the kitchen and blood all over the floor.

Calmly, I asked what had happened. When twelve-year-old Nina had picked up a cutting board, the handle had given way and the board had dropped down on her foot, cutting a deep gash in her second toe and breaking the toenail in half.

I sat her in a chair and placed my hands on her head. Heat of magnificent proportions was radiating from her and I had to gasp a breath of air (because I could feel her intense throbbing, pain, and fear). For approximately two minutes, I kept my hands on her head. I then knelt before her and placed my hands about two inches away from her toe. I closed my eyes and asked her to close her eyes too. I asked her to tell me when she could see a pinpoint of white light in her vision.

After she saw the white light, I asked her to tell me when she saw a purple light. Only moments passed and she said, "I see purple now." I asked, "How is the pain?" Nina replied, "It's gone." I removed my hands and the skin had resealed itself, with no more bleeding and no need for stitches.

The kids' eyes were as wide as saucers and they asked in a daze,

"What just happened?" Tiffany and Brandy, my nieces, aged six-teen and thirteen, replied, "Oh, this is our Aunt Gloria. She's a spiritual healer and she does miracles all the time."

A twelve-year-old boy named Matt came up to me moments later and said, "My back hurts all the time and my parents won't take me to the doctor. I jumped on Brandy's trampoline this morn-ing and I really hurt my back badly, can you heal me, too?" I asked him to lie on the floor and used my hands to energy-sense his back for hot and cold spots. On the left-hand side, below the rib cage, I could "see" that the energy wasn't flowing properly. Intuitively, I knew that it stemmed from the base of his neck. I placed my left hand on his back and my right hand on his neck.

I asked him to close his eyes and tell me when he saw the pin-point of white light in his vision. He did immediately. I asked him to tell me when he saw the purple light and within seconds, he said, "I can see it. It's beautiful and it's just waving and waving and waving." I asked him how his pain was and, as he stood, he twisted from side-to-side and repeated, "It doesn't hurt anymore, it doesn't hurt anymore. Thank you, thank you, thank you."

I then taught all the kids how to heal their own pain or an-other's. They were able to do it and so will you be.

When Danielle was in first grade, I was lying with her at bed-time talking about her day. She mentioned a tummy ache and she asked if I would do some energy work on her. I reminded her that she could do it herself. Danielle rubbed her hands and placed them on her stomach, closed her eyes and told me when she saw the white light, followed with the violet. Very quietly she said, "Mom, I'm a healer, too." I asked, "Danielle, did an inner voice just tell you that?" Softly she replied, "No, but the pain just went away."

Years have passed and I asked Danielle if she continues to see colors and she responds, "No, now it's just a feeling I have."

I have a feeling, also. I feel like everyone on this planet is de-serving of this information. I'll share my awareness, then the rest of it is up to you and God.

CHAPTER 7

When we surrender human judgment,
healing our minds,
we (re)discover our oneness
and therein lies our miracle

Before we drive downtown to the post office to pick up Miracle Publishing's mail, I want to show you a special scrapbook. As you will see, there are nearly thirty-six pictures of a woman taken over the course of the last eleven years. Even if I didn't have years of miracles to talk about, if this situation was the only one of which I had to speak, it could keep the interest of the highly religious as well as the devout atheists. The story begins on May 29, 1990, when I received a letter from a California State inmate, Linda K. Fudge, street name Nikki. The letter revealed a tragic lifestyle. Nikki had heard about me through the daughter of a friend of mine and found herself reaching out to me from prison.

She was going through heroin withdrawal, and had failed in a suicide attempt. The emergency room doctors at County Hospital ignored her pleas for help, believing them to be a ploy for more drugs. Because the hospital rejected her obvious injuries, the jail medical staff and officers ignored them as well.

The day I received her letter, I held it and meditated in order to be used as an instrument by spirit to share what Nikki most needed to hear. Seven pages evolved from that meditation, along with a three-page personal letter from me, accompanying the inspirational message.

In my letter to this woman, I shared that, though she was in an extremely negative environment, she could imagine a little miniature angel sitting on her shoulder, an angel who wasn't limited by a physical body and who could do anything. I mailed the ten pages immediately to Nikki.

By the way, I felt she was trying to gross me out with her lifestyle, through an unconscious desire to have me ignore her request, to ultimately prove that no one truly cared, and that she deserved all this suffering life had handed her.

Nikki received my letter and found herself responding immediately. She had made a card and drawn a self-portrait of herself in soft pastels. Her long hair was flowing, her eyes clear and beautiful, her breasts were the clouds, and sitting upon her shoulder was a tiny angel. Inside this card, she expressed her heartfelt gratitude.

The day I received this, I had the "rock 'em, sock 'em, knock you off your barstool, intuitive thunder of silence" telling me that Nikki was supposed to be the illustrator for the adult fairy-tale book that I had just completed, *To Become as Little Children,* or the *Tales.* I let no grass grow under my feet as I sent a second letter back to Nikki, asking—okay, maybe begging—her to consider being the illustrator for the *Tales.* Just as quickly, she responded affirmatively that she wanted to join in my dream.

Over the last fifteen years, I have written hundreds and hundreds of "Personalized Fairy Tales, Unlimited" for friends, family, strangers, and myself. People have always tended to treat me like the friendly neighborhood priest, sharing the troubles, heartaches, and experiences that they are too embarrassed to share with church-affiliated people.

I discovered long ago that once I hear a person's story, a fairy-tale title appears in my thoughts. If I have a title, I have a complete story for the individual, woven with spiritual metaphors and always concluding with a *happily-ever-after* new beginning. Sorting through a decade of hundreds of short stories I'd written, I chose forty-five tales that had universal appeal and combined them into book form. The subjects touch each of us, concerning every day of our lives.

Nikki was invited to illustrate the jacket for the *Tales,* and to do ten text illustrations. She had four colored pencils as she began the work, but, as she was being transferred from one prison to another, the guards confiscated her pencils. Nikki told me that she literally begged them not to take her pencils, explaining how important this project was. The guards responded, "Tough," and took them anyway. When she got to the new prison where she would remain for the next four years, she explained to the inmates what she was attempting to do and they borrowed colored pencils so she could continue the project.

Together, Nikki and I wrote a book, *Between Saint and Sinner*, that will touch the hearts of the masses whether locked behind doors or bars. Our friendship has spanned eleven years now and during that time she was paroled in my care and came to Montana to live with my family. For two years, we lived our long-awaited dream. Afterward, she became strong enough to live on her own. We remain best friends even today.

Thanks to Nikki, I was able to reach out to inmates across the nation. Miracle Publishing Company donated books to state and federal prisons to help men and women heal their lives.

I was even invited into the largest female prison in the United States, to speak to thirty-five inmates on the first of a two-day visit. We made a video of this occasion, but it did not receive approval for release to me and the outside world because "of all the touching and hugging" that day in prison. Such acts are not allowed behind bars. I explained to the warden that the women would never be frightened, threatened, or shamed out of their addictive behaviors. Rather, it would take awareness and perhaps spiritual healers to teach them.

From my first day's teachings, word had spread like wildfire that I'd be returning. For my second day, women lined up. Several inmates pleaded for a "healing hug," affirming that following it, they knew they'd be okay. I hugged each and every willing woman, placing my arms around them and whispering, "And don't let go until I tell you." I would close my eyes, placing my right hand on the back of their head and "scanning" their back with my left hand. When I saw the inner white Light, I released them, knowing that their entire lives were going to change.

During my second day, I stood before convicts, the warden, and the alumni reading a condensed version of Nikki's and my book, *Between Saint and Sinner*, which was written in fairy-tale form. At one point, I had to stop reading because the part of the tale I was reciting was extremely emotional to me. I apologized to the group. "I can't read this. Every single time I read this part, I break down crying because I love Nikki so very much." One of the inmates chided me from the audience saying, "Big deal if you cry! You've held us for two entire days while we cried in your arms. Read the damned fairy tale!"

I continued to read and broke into complete sobs, as promised. A lifer walked to my side, placed her arms around me with a heart-to-heart hug, and whispered, "And don't let go until I tell ya."

What I did for Nikki was to see something that already existed within her, long before we ever met. *Not something I created, something that was already there.*

In a letter written to me from prison she shared these thoughts: "You know, I was thinking about all that you took upon yourself in regards to me . . . all of the thousands of things in the last six years we've been best friends. I can't count it all, Gloria. As soon as I think I get close, another memory pops up . . . gifts surface on more than the material level, also. My spirit . . . my mind . . . my talent . . . my physical well being . . . my imagination . . . my heart . . . my emotional growth . . . my self esteem . . . on and on.

"Our relationship has touched and made better every single part of me that I am aware of and probably (certainly) parts I've yet to say hello to. You're a pretty marvelous best buddy, I hope you know. Well, it doesn't matter if you do, because I do and I'll find many, many ways to let you know that I know. And once I'm firmly placed in my working, earning capacity . . . stamps will be on me for the next fifteen to twenty years!"

This woman who chose to walk the hard road has touched the lives of thousands. When you see the beauty of her illustrations, you touch the beauty of her soul; you touch her robe.

Once, standing before a group of people, I shared Nikki's and my story, our miracles, and our lives as two individuals whose worlds had collided. I told them of the book we had coauthored, sharing that I am a sinner and Nikki is a saint. Normally, when speaking, I refer to myself as the saint and to her as the sinner.

I immediately felt judgments come from the audience, even though they were aware that they had come to hear a spiritual healer speak and teach. Just as society and the churches have judged Nikki a sinner, I, as a healer, have been judged and threatened. I guess it doesn't much matter which path one chooses to walk, until society becomes free of the judgments.

In one chapter Nikki tells about her life as a heroin addict, a habit she supported by prostitution. The following chapter is about me performing miracles in the local spa. The next chapter reveals how Nikki was raped and that is followed with more miracles. Somewhere within the pages, we reverse roles and Nikki becomes the teacher while I adopt the role of the student, unveiling my shadows before the reader.

The moral of our story and lives is that we are both the saint and sinner and we are both neither. We are just two people doing the best we can with the awareness we have. When we surrender human judgment, healing our minds, we (re)discover our oneness and therein lies our miracle.

CHAPTER 8

I can *heal my life*

As you can see, I get a lot of fan mail, and I am still personally answering every individual letter. There are more messages on the recorder, also, which I will need to respond to, but I'd like to finish what we've started first.

A man once called me long distance, requesting a healing from cancer. His doctors had given him a death sentence, stating that they had done all they could do. He had heard about me through a friend of a friend of a friend.

When he told me he had cancer, I responded by saying, "This is your lucky day, because I don't believe in cancer!" He asked how much I charged and I said, "Normally, I don't, but with you, it's going to cost you. In fact, it's going to cost you big time!" He questioned meekly, "How much?" My voice got soft as I said, "One more long distance phone call, to tell me, after you go to your doctor again, that your cancer has gone into remission." He called again and voiced those exact words to me.

A doctor once told me that I had breast cancer and I responded, "I can heal my life." The doctor's voice got stern as he said, "No, you don't understand. You have breast cancer." With all the authority I could muster, I countered with, *"No, you don't understand. I can heal my life!"* (And so I did.)

Approximately seven years ago, every single hair fell from my head. Three professionals told me that the follicles were dead and that my hair would never grow back. To each, I said, "You just watch me!" As I was sitting Indian-style before a full-length mirror one morning I said aloud to God, "If there's a secret to making my hair grow back in, I need to know it now!" Immediately, the telephone rang and it was my six-foot-tall friend and neighbor, Michelle. She asked if I'd like to run errands with her and I agreed to join her.

Our last stop was at a metaphysical bookstore in Sacramento. I stepped over the threshold and across the room I could see an orange book on the top shelf. I said, "Michelle, I don't know what that book is, but I *need* it. Please bring it down for me."

The book opened at random to chapter 56 and, I cross my heart and swear to God, in bold print it said, "If you're looking for the secret to falling hair, here it is." It was a hand reflexology book and it said to briskly rub the fingernails of each hand together, doing this three times a day for at least five minutes. I began immediately and, as soon as I did, it felt like the top of my head had caught on fire!

Over the next few days, where handfuls of hair had fallen out in various patterns on my skull, a five o'clock shadow was appearing. Within less than two weeks, I had a five o'clock shadow on my entire head. The following morning, poof . . . through so-called dead follicles, hair grew through the shafts and today, I have a full and complete head of hair. It really works. I'm proof.

It probably sounds as though I don't have a high regard for the medical profession. That isn't true. My grandmother was a doctor and she along with two other doctors called me into their professional offices to give assistance when the medical world couldn't do any more. I believe that, even with their limited methods, they do serve the masses. However, those who find their way to me are those who are tired of being used as guinea pigs or of hearing from the doctors, "I don't know what's wrong, but let's try this." There are also those who are tired of paying for expensive medication that only masks, but does not heal, the true underlying cause. Our awareness/consciousness is rising, however, and one day, doctors and spiritual healers may join hands to achieve the best of both worlds.

My mother used to call me from Denver, weekly, with names of people who needed healings. One Friday evening she called with news that hit home. My sister, Sheila, had taken the nieces and nephews roller-skating. She knew she was going to fall so she braced herself and when she fell, she shattered her elbow.

While my mom was sharing the event, I could hear the sound of the Holy Spirit breathing, reverberating throughout my dining room and I couldn't catch my breath. Momentarily, I thought that perhaps I was dying but if so, it wasn't frightening, just a little uncomfortable because I couldn't breathe. I asked my mom if I should call her back after this passed and she said, "No-o-o, out of concern for your safety, I'm going to stay on the phone."

Only milliseconds passed and I said, "Mom, I don't know what just happened, but I think Sheila's going to be okay." Seventy-two hours passed and my mom called again. She gave me names of more people to be healed and, just before she hung up, she nonchalantly added, "Oh, and by the way, today at work, Sheila's arm swelled up under her cast and was hurting her real badly. After work, she went to the doctor. They cut her cast away and, Gloria, her arm is healed."

To be honest, I don't know why it takes seventy-two hours for some miracles to be made manifest. I know that after the crucifixion, it took three days before the stone was rolled away from the tomb. I have no idea whether seventy-two hours is a significant period of time for the physical body to become a spiritual body or what the connection may be. If that's one of your questions, meditate on it, contemplate it, and get back to me with the answer!

I don't keep track of miracles, or that would be about all I would get done. Some stick out in my mind, not because they were harder, but because of the circumstances.

A man who had AIDS heard about me through his cousin. He was nearing death and was so very sick that it took him two months to come to my home. He was skeptical, but he had nothing to lose. After I had seen him twice, his physician asked him, "What is the *one* thing you're doing that your six dead friends didn't do?" The man responded that he was seeing me. His doctor said, "Well, I'm skeptical, but don't stop seeing her!"

After the man's fourth visit, tests were taken, and I've been told that it's been medically documented that he no longer has AIDS. His physician would like to meet me. It seems that the doctor has a female patient, a thirty-four-year-old woman who has AIDS. The woman's concern is not for herself, or her recovery, but for her four-year-old daughter, as there is no one to leave her with if she dies. The doctor said, "Maybe Gloria would be able to help this woman, too." An open-minded, open-hearted doctor!

The healed man shared, "Where there was no hope before, AIDS patients now have something to look forward to." But he has not openly shared my name with others who have the virus. He explained, "If others knew, you would be inundated with just those who carry the virus." Instead, he has learned the technique, sharing individually and at AIDS support groups. The ripple effect will mirror itself globally.

I heard of a man in Virginia who had a heart birth defect. The Walter Reed Army Hospital in Washington, D.C., had documented his condition for ten years. He was being prepared for surgery to have the heart valve of a pig grafted onto his heart. I heard of his situation through his wife and was introduced to him by telephone. That evening, with his permission, I laid my hands on my heart, closed my eyes, and saw the Light. I asked for peace and felt two electric shocks. I knew the man was healed.

He subsequently saw a specialist, tests were run, and he was told that his heart was in the high-to-normal range and asked to come back in November to be tested again, just to be on the safe side. I encourage all people to continue with medical care, even if they are receiving spiritual healing.

Angela had heard of me through the grapevine and called asking to see me. When her husband brought her to my home, Angela took slow steps with her walker. I treated her for approximately twenty minutes. I could telepathically hear her husband's judgments and skepticism.

After the treatment, we were discussing my healing ability. He said, "It's not that I don't believe in miracles, because I do. It's just that . . ." (As he paused, I felt it necessary to fill in the blanks.) "It's just that you've never really met anyone who could actually do it, right?" He confirmed my statement.

He continued, "I'm from Missouri." I asked, "You mean from the Bible Belt?" He retorted, "No, from the Show-Me State. You show me and I'll believe." Teasing, I said, "Great idea, next week, bring your wife back to me. You show me yours and I'll show you mine!"

I explained to him and I explain to you now. I understand. Oh, God, I understand so well. The hesitation or fears of others do not offend me, because I understand so much more than they could ever begin to believe. I was skeptical, too. In fact, I praise your discernment. I would hate to think that people would be so gullible as to just believe anyone's words. Allow the demonstrations that occur through me to be the proof that what I teach and speak is true. If I wasn't a spiritual healer myself, I don't know "if I would believe it." This is why it's so important for everyone to learn how to do this themselves. Trusting in God, being used as His instrument, you can lay hands on your child, on your spouse, or on yourself and feel the power of spirit working through you.

Shortly after I saw Angela, she called me on the telephone with fear in her voice. She pleaded with me on the answering machine to return her phone call. She needed the assurance of hearing me tell her that pain in her arm, leg, and shoulder where I had worked was okay. I returned her call as soon as I heard the message. I questioned, "How long ago was it that you felt that side of your body?" Angela hesitated and said, "My gosh, it was eleven years ago, before I had my stroke!" I replied, "I think we should look upon the pain as a blessing. That side of your body is coming back to life."

The following week, Angela returned, not with a walker, but with a claw-foot cane. The third time she came back, the claw-foot cane was replaced with "just a plain ol' cane." Mostly for swinging, I'd say! Her right shoulder, which had slipped out of the socket eleven years before, had now gone back in place and reset itself. Her heel had been frozen into such a position that she had been walking on the toes of the right foot, but now she walked normally again. As Angela hugged me, she swept her hands down her body and said, "I don't even care about any of this. I have my mind back again!"

Angela continues to use and demonstrate these teachings to heal herself, as well as teaching others how to do so. Her husband believes in me, as well as in himself, now. He successfully used the technique after shutting a window on his finger. He doesn't want my gift turned into a "dog and pony show" and has found himself standing and speaking with authority, on my behalf concerning who I am and what I do. Will miracles just never cease?

CHAPTER 9

I will hold you up in the Light and I will support you in any way I can to help others

Would you please join me at the local store to get groceries before I have to go pick up the kids from school? I make a menu for each week so, while at the store, I'm organized and don't forget anything I'll need for the entire week. I'd also like to rent a movie for the kids. Tonight is a special evening. They're getting their report cards and I'd like to reward them for their good grades and effort.

Speaking of movies, as a family, we don't rent movies that promote fear or insanity in the world. We also limit the television programs we watch so the kids aren't brainwashed into believing that insanity is acceptable.

It takes a lot of energy to be consistent, raising kids. Kirk and I are extremely family oriented and do our very best to listen to our kids, to truly hear what they have to say. We encourage them to do their best at whatever it is they enjoy doing. We believe that the support of a healthy family is the foundation on which the world's healing will occur. It must always begin within the home.

Years ago, in 1985, when all the spiritual experiences began occurring with me, one of the first messages I ever received from spirit was, "If your children ever need you, you are to stop immediately whatever you're doing and answer the call." Not only did it balance out the incredible supernatural events that were occurring

47

in my life at that time, but it also bonded me more closely to the children, showing me what is most important.

Some have made the judgment against me that I really don't know what is truly going on in the world. Granted, I rarely read the newspapers or watch the news. I've responded, in such cases, "In order to be an effective spiritual healer, I can't have prejudgments of what's good or bad that's going on in the world." It doesn't take a genius to figure out that the promotion of negative events is the only sensational thing that gets people's attention. I don't buy into it for a second.

I'm not asking you to bury your head in the sand, go into denial, or ignore the insanity on this planet. I'm also not asking you to see beauty if it's ugliness that surrounds you. We are not trying to change a human's bad perspective or experience into a human good experience. We must rise above both and that can only be accomplished by seeking the Light and allowing it to dissolve the human errors of miscreation.

If you find yourself enjoying the evening paper and the ten o'clock news, discovering dishonest situations, destruction, or insanity in various forms, then, upon retiring, call forth the Light to bring peace into your awareness of that situation. World peace, it's a dream—yours and mine. Together, with this valid information, we can make it reality.

I've had people ask me, If you can truly do all that you say you do, why don't you go to work in a children's hospital? The same woman who called me an Angel of Satan, was asking this question of me. It took me several minutes to get over the initial shock and hurt. My response to her was this, "I've spent two hours sharing what has happened to and through me over the years and you do not trust me. How do you propose that I go into a hospital and attempt to convince the authorities to permit me to do a healing service?" She truly couldn't answer the question. (Now, however, as an ordained minister, I can legally call upon those in hospitals and institutions.)

The gift of healing can appear to be a threat. If I teach people how to heal their lives, there will be no more need for hospitals, nurses, doctors, lab technicians, medical insurance, drug companies, cafeteria personnel, cleaners, etc. Sick people are good for profits. Sick people make a sick society, however, and ultimately, a sick world. Where are our priorities? I am willing to teach the doctors how to do what I do, to empower them. That, in my future days to come, may just be the ticket.

By the way, while we're in the grocery store, you're going to notice that practically everyone knows me by name. That is not because I'm some world-famous author or healer, but because I'm an individual in this town who always has a smile on my face, a kind word to speak, and bells on my shoes. Yes, don't forget the bells!

You might ask why a grown woman wears bells on her shoes? Years and years ago, I watched, *It's a Wonderful Life* with Jimmy Stewart. The angel, Clarence, told Jimmy that "every time a bell rings, an angel gets his wings." It's my belief that we need as many angels as we can get, at this point in Earth's evolution to a spiritual planet. I've got to be honest though, I love to attract attention, too! The other day while shopping, I ran across sleigh bells and I was incredibly tempted to buy them. While in the store, I placed one huge bell, which was actually bigger than my shoe on each shoe, and I walked around the store, listening to the magical music my feet were making. Only the thought of embarrassing my friends or family motivated me to put the sleigh bells back on the shelf.

My friend Nikki once told me that I'd be great before the cameras of television or on stage in front of hundreds or thousands of people. Thinking she had had a revelation or vision concerning me, I couldn't wait to hear more. Then her human honesty entered the picture as she concluded, "Because you don't mind making an ass of yourself."

Well, that's not totally true. I do embarrass myself at times. But, for the most part, I've grown to the level that I really don't care what people think. I love and accept myself in spite of my addictions, fears, weaknesses, and inferiority complex. (Just like you, I heal my life on a daily basis.) There are times that I still seek the approval of the world, but those times are becoming fewer and fewer. I explain to people that I've been confirmed by God and I don't need their approval.

One of the ways I recently embarrassed myself was after talking before hundreds of people as a motivational speaker. Afterward, as usual, the crowd gathered around and lined up for healing hugs. I know certain things as I'm hugging or focused on people. I just do! While hugging a woman, I found myself saying, "You're starving yourself to death. Knock it the hell off!" We parted from the embrace and she smiled genuinely and lovingly at me, responding, "You're right."

Two weeks later, I was back in this same city doing individual one-on-one healings. The above-mentioned woman was my last appointment on the first day. As she entered the room, she introduced herself as Dominique, reminding me of what I'd said during our healing hug. She asked if I remembered her and I said, "Of course I do."

I began the process of healing and found myself kneeling before her, with my hands on her stomach area. I also have the gift of being able to see through the skin, to see the energy patterns within a person. I can see where the energy is blocked and am then able to reopen the channels so that healing can occur. (I always teasingly say, "Superman thinks he's so smart because he can see through clothes, but nanner-nanner, I can see beyond the skin.") I'm a human X-ray machine.

As the story goes, I could see so many blockages within Dominique and then I knew why she was starving herself to death. It was not a conscious choice or desire of her own. She had blockages that created a feeling of "fullness." When she would eat, she would be unable to eliminate the waste properly.

As I knelt before her, with my eyes closed looking within her, Dominique quietly stated, "I'm a sister of the Catholic Order." Without opening my eyes, I questioned, "Then where is your habit?" She giggled and said, "We gave them up years ago." Showing my quick wit, I responded, "Whoopi Goldberg still wears hers!" The sister and I both got a laugh out of that comment. But, for me, the laughter helped to cover up the embarrassment I felt because of the comment I'd made during our first meeting. (I had to trust that she had needed to hear those words.)

Before I arose from the kneeling position, this beautiful woman, who has a heart of gold, placed her hands upon my head. Sister

Dominique said, "I bless you, Gloria. I will hold you up in the Light and I will support you in any way that I can to help others." My friend, I was totally and completely touched (by the Hands of God!) I felt as though her actual words were those of the Holy Spirit!

Before we said our good-byes that evening, the sister told me that from the moment she had seen my face in the featured article of the newspaper, she had known "I was real." Dominique had come to the group to hear me speak, to watch me from the side-lines. As I came into contact with each individual, she witnessed that I was kind and loving to everyone, no matter who they were. She added, "That was the compassion of God flowing through you, Gloria."

I do love people. In fact, love or the miracles that flow from it is something that I'd be unable to fake. I can't even fake a speech. I never pre-plan what I will say when standing before others.

Once, I had been invited to be a guest speaker to a congregation of people. I opened the speech with the two lines that were in my thoughts and then I looked into the group's eyes and the room fell silent. No thoughts. No speech. Just dead silence. I asked the congregation if they had questions. (Perhaps if they asked questions, it would steer me in the direction to take.) Who has ever been brought in as a motivational speaker, only to stand before a group and say, I have nothing to say? Me. The speech then began flowing, as guided by spirit. I'm telling you honestly, of myself, I can do nothing. Yes, my friend, "I'm real" and I enjoy being a spiritual-human being!

All my promotional materials are in the trunk of my car, so we'll need to put the groceries in the backseat. The family is going to enjoy this movie I got for them. If you would like to stick around for dinner, you could watch it with us if there's time. It's the Santa Claus Movie with Tim-the-Tool-Man-Taylor, which has become part of our holiday tradition. The whole family watched it when it was released, and it was after seeing this movie that I discovered that I look like an elf!

When we returned from the movie, I caught my reflection in a mirror and said, "Kirk, I look like an elf," and he responded immediately, "I know." I continued, "No, I mean it! I have fat cheeks, short hair, wear bells on my shoes, I wear tiny stretch pants, and huge shirts." (It was as if I'd had a major revelation!) Almost as if I was trying to convince Kirk, I shrieked, "I'm serious, I look like an elf!" Again, he flatly repeated, "I know."

I called my sister, Sheila, and told her, also. Casually, she responded, "I know." I asked, "If everyone knew this, why didn't someone tell me?" She replied, "We all thought you knew. It would be like telling you that you had brown eyes."

Another thing I need to share is that Kirk and I believe in discipline. Children need to be disciplined and they need consistency. However, I don't believe in hitting. I believe that you can set them on a time-out for not doing a good job listening, you can send them to their rooms, you can ground them from the phone and friends and even take the car keys from them. If all that fails, then hit 'em! (Just kidding! Just seeing if you're paying attention!)

Truthfully, as you learn to plug in to the source directly, and achieve a peaceful state of mind, that emotion will flow outwardly to others in your everyday life. That includes your immediate family members, your home and office environment, neighbors, county, city, and state. Once again, the ripple effect becomes global.

We have about an hour before we go get the kids from school, and I'd like to take that time to show you something very special to me. I think you'll enjoy it, too.

Enter, please if you will, my master bedroom. You'll see on my dresser some little ceramic Hands of God that my sister, Sheila, made for me years ago. Years before I ever became spiritual. Over the last fifteen years, I have placed the names or photos of people in God's hands to be healed. Also, please notice all the brown paper bag lunch sacks near my dresser. There are now too many names to actually place each one separately in His ceramic hands as I always used to. Now I place them next to His hands within the sacks.

I'd like you to feel something, so please hold out your hand. This is a cross and chain, made of pure silver, which I was recently given while out on a promotional trip in the Northwest. It's not the silver that I want you to feel. Instead, feel the love that inspired the giving.

I had stood before a group of hundreds of people that night, sharing that I had touched everyone I knew (and many I didn't know) with this healing gift. However, there have been many long days and nights when I opened myself to the universal stream of pure love and there was no one present to receive the gift.

I explained to the audience that having this gift and no one to share it with is like owning a candy store and finding everyone on a diet. I need to be used, first and foremost by God, and then by others. (I've given a new meaning to the word *used*, haven't I?)

Healing others or myself doesn't drain me, because it's not my energy. My humility is not false. If I were to believe it is my energy, as a human, I would be limited in how many I could help. By knowing that it's God's unlimited energy, I can draw upon it without exhausting the supply or myself. Also, if I thought the words that write the books were mine, they would neither heal, nor sell. All attempts to do so would be limited. If I, on an ego level, believed myself to be a great healer or author, the gifts would be diminished and I would find myself helping no one.

CHAPTER 10

*Any gift given without love
is worthless*

I always explain that I might not have personal time for each and every individual I meet. But, if people will write their names or the names of loved ones on paper and seal them in envelopes, I will take them back to Montana with me and do the healing long distance.

When I returned home from that weekend, it took me all morning to open the envelopes. Inside were financial donations (which I had never before received in ten years of doing this) and there were also Christmas ornaments and jewelry. I was completely and totally overwhelmed with all that I had been given.

The silver cross was in one envelope, along with a note saying that the owner had had this necklace most of her life. I cried. This person, who may not have had any money to give, gave in the greatest way of all, through a demonstration of selfless love.

My first day back from this trip, it took me most of the day to finish up all the business and to do my regular chores. The following day, as I was having coffee with Kirk, he asked me, "What do you have planned to do today?" I said, "I have a little more business to take care of, as well as laundry. Why, do you need me to do some errands for you?" He replied, "No, but at one o'clock today, I'd like you to turn off the phone, close the drapes, lock the door, and begin healing all those people whose names you brought back with you." (I almost cried again! I am blessed to have such loving support and understanding from my mate.)

At one o'clock that afternoon, I did as Kirk had suggested. I came into the bedroom and got the sack of over five hundred names. For a moment, I felt overwhelmed. I didn't have time to take each person individually into the Light.

A calming thought entered and I laid down on the couch, rubbed my hands together, placed the entire envelope on my heart center, and placed my healing hands on top of the sack. Immediately, it felt like my heart center opened to the size of the Grand Canyon and in flowed the liquid light and loving warmth, the presence of God.

The powerful but gentle energy flowed down into the tips of my toes, flooding its way up my legs, filling the entire Grand Canyon. It felt like every single cell of mine was singing. A bold voice from within said, "You're not healing five hundred people, Gloria, you're healing one belief that there's a power in opposition to Me. Be at peace!"

For the following two hours, I had hundreds of shifts and shocks in my body as those across the miles received their healing. I felt special to be a part of healing the masses.

Three national feature articles have been written about me. Following the articles, my phone began ringing until ten o'clock at night. Along with the calls came unheard of amounts of mail, many containing donations. I had no awareness of what to do with the money. I meditated and was guided to see a local accountant. He suggested that since I'm an ordained minister, I could set up a nonprofit organization and feed the donations into it. The foundation of Miracle Healing Ministry began. The ministry is providing for book donations to prisoners, and my travels to the prisons, churches, and auditoriums to give service to the mainstream of masses across the states.

God, through my individual consciousness, is providing. The outpouring of spirit is providing a vehicle, the speeches, the healings, the food, the people to help me, everything. I do, I do, I do believe in miracles!

Let me tell you just one more story and then we'll go get the kids from school. (I have so many. It's hard for me because I want to share them all right this minute.) Years ago, a man who was legally blind heard of me through a Unity Church and called, asking for a healing. I drove to his home and shared my "love Light" with him. I taught Jerry how to use this information every day for everything.

Seventy-two hours passed (here we go again . . .) and he called me saying, "Gloria, you know how it is when you walk in from a cold environment to a hot one and your glasses fog up?" I answered, "Yes." Jerry continued, "After several hours in the mall today, I was standing at the check-out line when this happened. I removed my glasses and I could read what was on the counter!" Joyfully he said, "I'm standing in the kitchen right now talking to you, but I can see across the room, to the clock on the living room wall, and I can tell you what time it is!" (Thanks, God!)

Months later, Jerry telephoned me again. He began the conversation by telling me that he'd had a dream about me the night before and that he had to share it. I listened as he shared the dream. Then he said, "I have several things I'm supposed to tell you. One of your next books is to be entitled, *Dream Catchers*, another fairy-tale book for adults." I interrupted him at this point, because he, himself, was an author of children's books. I said, "Jerry, that's a beautiful title! Why don't you use it?" He answered, "Because it's not mine, it's yours."

As he continued to speak, I could feel an intense love and strong energy behind his words. I listened as though it was the Creator personally talking to me. Jerry told me that my books were going to become extremely popular, and through that popularity, I might become famous. (I explained that this would be acceptable, but it certainly wasn't what I was seeking.)

Jerry ended the message of the dream with, "Though so many wonderful things are coming your way, the message is: Don't get cocky, don't get greedy and continue to give the glory to God."

I thanked Jerry for the message. I shared that because I know where all the miracles and experiences are coming from, and knowing my personality, I didn't think I had too much to worry about.

However, I thanked him again for sharing because, through the awareness, I would do my best to never allow that to happen. I concluded, "I'm not seeking glory, nor criticism. The glory can go to God and the criticism can go to hell."

Jerry's words, just like this necklace, were a gift given with love. I tell people that any gift given without love is worthless no matter the price. Sometimes I'm filled with so much love and if I find myself without another to give it to, it physically hurts my heart. I have to hug a tree or kiss a rock. Being what I am, I have to give all that I can. The more I give, the more I have to give. If things are stuck in your life, giving of yourself will reopen you to the infinite supply.

It's snowing now, and I promised to pick up the kids from school. I always arrive fifteen minutes early. I park under the trees and, as the kids walk by, I hear them talking about where the parties are, who's pregnant, who's getting an abortion, where you can get the drugs, etc. My kids think I'm psychic, imagine that!

CHAPTER 11

All you have to do is nothing;
and all I have to do,
is love you more than
you've ever been loved
before in your life

Don't roll your eyes at me, but sitting here at the school reminds me of a couple stories I'd like to share. Ten years ago, Kirk heard that I was divorcing. He asked me to come to Montana, offering me a place to heal my heart. We had been friends for eighteen years, but I didn't want to step out of one relationship right into another one. I kept asking God what I should do, and Kirk kept calling.

I had to be honest with him. I was seeking divine guidance about what to do with my two kids, and my service to Him, and myself. Kirk replied, "Gloria, you keep asking God what to do, but you need to listen. He's saying that you need to move to Montana!"

Kirk flew into Denver (where I was staying with my sister, Sheila) on August 23. On August 24, we rented a U-Haul, and on August 25, I followed a man I'd only seen once in eleven years to Montana. Outside of Billings, I had a panic attack. I silently screamed, *Gloria, what in the hell are you doing?* Kirk sensed it, though he was driving the U-Haul in front of me. He pulled off at a rest stop and held me, assuring me that everything was going to be fine.

He said he wouldn't rush me. He lied. Two months later, on

October 5 (my birthday), he proposed. Another two months later, on December 8 (his birthday), we married. Kirk has two daughters, Kerrie and Jaime, who became my stepdaughters. We've all dropped the "step" because it really isn't important. They continue to see and love their mother. I'm just "the other mom" who does the cooking, cleaning, listening, and nagging.

I hadn't seen Kerrie and Jaime since they were babies, so to move into a home with two built-in teenagers was all new to me. The first three days of school, before they left the home, Kerrie cried. On the third day, I had to ask her what the problem was. She explained, "I'm seventeen years old and I've never had a first date or a first kiss. It just saddens me to start my junior year and know that it's going to happen all over again!"

I couldn't believe my ears (or eyes). I was standing in the kitchen, looking at this beautiful girl who was telling me that she couldn't get a date? Surely she must be joking. I said, "Kerrie, you are beautiful, inside and out. You have the prettiest auburn hair I've ever seen, pretty eyes, a sweet smile, you're intelligent, a petite figure, and a wonderful personality! My God, you have it all!"

She just cried harder. If she had it all and still couldn't get a date, then something must be really horribly wrong with her, she thought.

I realized that she wasn't joking and an example came to my mind. I said, "Kerrie, for just a moment, I want you to envision two balloons attached to separate helium tanks. One balloons says, 'I can't get a date.' The other balloon says, 'I can get any guy I want!' Each thought you put on the balloon fills it with energy very rapidly, the balloon expands and pops, with the energy/belief/experience becoming part of your physical reality. Knowing this, where do you want to put your attention/energy/air?"

She felt better. There were no more tears before school. Seventy-two hours after I told Kerrie the balloon theory, there was a knock at our front door. It was a senior hunka-hunka-burnin' love, asking Kerrie to tutor him in algebra. The next night, he returned to be tutored in English. The third night, the "dumb bunny" (who was using this as an excuse to be around Kerrie) showed up in time for dinner and tutoring in another subject.

He asked her on a date. They started going steady. (That's my term. Teens call it "going out.") Kerrie got her first date and first kiss. (Of course, I had to ask for all the details!)

Kerrie later told me that she would forever be grateful. She believed that none of that would have ever happened if I hadn't moved to Montana.

Now, Jaime, there's another story! She's my little Earth Angel. When she was young, she dragged home more stray people than you can imagine.

When I first arrived in Montana, I noticed that whenever Jaime got angry at Kerrie, she would call her "brain dead." (You can just imagine how well that went over with me!) I tried to mind my own business. Really, I did! But, then I made it my business to take care of this situation.

I forewarned Jaime, "The next time you say something derogatory about Kerrie, I'm going to ask you to write and say ten nice things about her." She made the mistake of retorting, "*One* would be hard to come up with!" With great authority, I said, "Now you can write twenty nice things about your sister." She did. It became "Benish law" that no one was allowed to speak poorly of themselves or another under my roof or they would have to perform the activity mentioned above. Teenagers have such low self-esteem that I just couldn't allow this to continue.

One afternoon, Jaime brought a young man home and asked if he could stay for dinner. (I think it was a test just to see how loving Gloria really is.) Rob had long, greasy, grimy, gopher-gutty hair, and a black leather jacket. Need I say more? (I know, I know . . . the judgments! I told you that I'm also working on healing them as I become aware.)

I told Jaime he could stay, and then turned to Rob and asked, "Would you like to join us for dinner?" He said he'd love to. As I was preparing the meal, I could hear the two of them down in Jaime's room, playing her electric guitar.

While at dinner and making polite conversation, I enthusiastically said, "Rob, what a beautiful voice you have. What are you going to do with that talent?" Without hesitation, he responded, "Oh, I can't sing." I said, "Of course you can sing. I heard you. You sing beautifully, are you in a band?" Again, without hesitation and with a broken-spirited, low self-esteem tone, replied, "Oh, I'm not good enough to be in a band."

Here was a complete stranger. We had only met minutes before, so I was surprised to hear myself saying, "Rob, in this house, whenever we degrade ourselves, it's Benish law that we have to write ten nice things about ourselves." He snapped back with, "I'd be lucky if I could think of one!" I followed with, "That just cost you ten more. Tomorrow, after school, I'll be sitting in my car, parked under the tree, waiting for the kids. I want you to do your homework tonight and handwrite me twenty nice things about yourself to give to me tomorrow. Just be there."

He started to open his mouth to say something and Jaime said, "Rob, you'd better shut up. My mom's serious. She just won't stand for anyone degrading themselves in front of her!"

The following day, at 3:30 as promised, I was waiting at the school. I really didn't know whether Rob would follow my advice or not. He didn't know me, and he certainly didn't owe me anything. It was once again in God's hands.

At 3:40, Rob walked up to my car window with a canary yellow sheet of paper in his hand. He said, "Ya know, Gloria, I was awake all night long trying to think of twenty nice things about myself. I didn't get any sleep, but instead of feeling tired today, I feel great! Thanks so very much for caring." He handed me his homework and I gave him an A plus. (The latest word has it that Rob is working in Alaska, and doing very well.)

Oh, there's D.W., Danielle, and Danielle's friend, Chelsea, coming now! After we get home and hear about their day, I'll let them begin the movie. I'm then going to give you some one-on-one attention, an experience of my gift. Don't be nervous—all you have to do is nothing and all I have to do is love you more than you've ever been loved before in your life.

CHAPTER 12

If you've got God, you've got it all

This may sound confusing, but before we're finished you will understand. It's not because I'm a "nice person" that I'm able to perform miracles. It's because I perform miracles that I'm a nice person. Me being a good human being has nothing to do with the gifts I've become aware of or have been given. I know you're going to think this is weird, but I don't have health because my heart, liver, and lungs are healthy. It sounds amazingly mystical, I know, but I don't depend upon any of those vital organs to live. (Call me opti-mystic.)

Remember when I told you that the presence of God had said that He didn't look to man, nor Earth to support Him? He didn't depend upon a heart or lungs to sustain His life. Nor do I. I'm sure you believe that now I've gone just too damned far! I can hear y'all saying about now, Well, let's just see how long you'd live if your heart didn't beat and your lungs didn't supply oxygen, and without that blood, you'd be graveyard dead.

On a physical level, yes, you're right, but would you rather be right or happy? As a healer, I'm not seeking to heal your heart or lungs (or my own). I'm focusing on healing the mind, purifying the state of consciousness and, when that occurs, you have the spiritual health made manifest through the lungs, heart, and through every single cell of your being.

During one of my visits to a women's prison, on the first day I noticed a woman sitting quietly in the back of the room, facing the wall. She didn't want to be on video, she didn't want a healing hug, she didn't want any part of the experience. I didn't take it personally.

I had been told that the woman was retarded. She had killed her child and the inmates weren't sure if she mentaly "lost it" after she did that or if she had been like that before this had contributed to her committing the crime. At any rate, this woman never spoke to anyone. Throughout that first day, she sat quietly alone. Before I left the prison on the first day, I asked her again if she would like a hug. She shook her head no and walked away looking at the ground.

The following day, I was to speak before the warden, the alumni, and the inmates. Just before I began speaking, this same woman asked the man who had organized my trip into the prison if she, herself, could say a few words after I finished. Of course, he was delighted to let her do this.

When I had finished speaking, the entire room became silent as this inmate approached the podium. Her speech was brief. With confidence and a voice filled with sincerity, she said, "If you've got God, you've got it all." She walked directly to me for a heart-to-heart hug and she cried in my arms.

In eight words, this inmate had said what I'm attempting to teach everyone. Daily, as you open your mind to that violet Light, it is the activity of God, the very presence of God that will lead you to whatever you need. It may lead you to the right book (which you open at random), where you will discover the answer to your question. It goes before you and prepares the perfect parking space or the airline ticket you need. The Light attracts the perfect mate into your life, allowing you a spiritual relationship based on healthy, happy experiences. Without affirming or taking human thought, the Light floods your life with abundance, health, joy, success, and peace. The Light is all in all.

I had a friend ask me recently, "Why you? Why is your life so perfect? I mean, I'm glad you're happy, but you could have a stinky home life and still have a successful career. As it is, you've got the beautiful, perfect family and everything else outside of that. Why you?" Well, my friend, why not you?

For me to be labeled as a spiritual healer means nothing, really. I, Gloria, am not the healer. My consciousness of God is the healing agent. However, in providing my mind to be used by spirit as the instrument through which the healings occur takes a twenty-four-hour-a-day dedication and devotion.

I have a passion within me to seek the Light, to love others, and to write of the miracles. I'm not a literary giant and I definitely don't have all the correct grammar. However, I have plenty to share if you can see beyond my human flaws. In 1985, I had my union with God. In that moment, I made a vow that the things of this earth no longer mattered to me. My only true desire was to experience the fullness of God. To become a healer for the masses and to carry more Light than the average human, I spent anywhere from eight to ten hours a day absorbing the Light. You, as an individual in this world and raising kids and/or working for a living, do not need to dedicate eight hours a day.

What I do is not for a living, but a loving: a loving passion for humanity and God. You are able to do what I do by merely spending the first few minutes of the day in the Light. As you continue to see the changes in your outer, day-to-day world, you might then begin devoting the first few minutes of each hour in seeking the Light. The expansion of your consciousness will accelerate and demonstrate the spiritual reality.

I have devoted my life to service in healing, writing, and nurturing my children and you. It's my purpose. It's the divine plan of my life. Yours will soon be revealed.

Several years ago, my friend June had the opportunity to go with me on a four-day promotional weekend. Three of the days would be spent doing individual, private healings and the fourth day would be spent in teaching an all-day healing workshop. I'll use just one of those days as an example. I awoke at 5:00 A.M., and went into the Light (meaning I opened my mind to the Light that is already within). I then spent the entire day healing individuals, many of whom were emotional or filled with extreme pain.

After finishing, around 7:30 P.M., June and I went to a restaurant. It was busy and it took quite a while for us to be served. Following dinner, I needed to fuel my car so I would be ready the next morning to drive the ninety miles to where the workshop was being held (it began at 9:00 A.M., so it would be another early morning).

I arrived back at the hostess's home at 10:20 P.M., discovering that I needed to make a call to the man who was arranging the workshop. We spoke until 10:40 P.M. I said, "June, I have twenty minutes before I head to bed, so that I can open myself to the Light, to be used throughout the night for those seeking healings." June then understood the devotion it takes to be a spiritual healer at this level of consciousness. My mind and body are no longer mine. They belong to God. This information is given to heal your life and those near and dear to you. If you are drawn to heal the masses, you will know the passion of which I speak.

To individually heal your mind is not a mental process. Metaphysically and on a karmic (cause and effect) level, you could affirm and program your subconscious for forty days and forty nights and sooner or later, it might become a part of your outer experience. Whether it does or not depends upon two things: your fears and your desires. Your fears will block your good and if you desire something too strongly, since we're electromagnetic energy, you will repel your good if you aren't careful. It's a dilemma, no?

The perfect healing only comes from a purified state of consciousness. The light dissolves the fear, pain, doubt, uncertainty, hate, and judgment. I will repeat myself as often as necessary: Once the human judgment is healed (purified by the Light) your outer world of appearance changes.

Join me in the living room. That's where I take visitors so I can do the healings.

Within this room, as you can see, the plants are growing like crazy. They love all the Light that gets channeled into the physical and they absorb it. I talk to my plants and tell them how lovely they are, but, as you can see, they are beautiful. So, of course, they should be told. We should never hold on to a compliment. We should give them as freely as they come to mind.

Like I said earlier, all you have to do is nothing and all I have to do is love you more than you've ever been loved before in your life. I'm not talking about human love because human love can be conditioned or withheld. Unconditional love is the pure energy of which we are all created. God recently said to me, "You are created in My image, held within My imagination, within My divine mind where you are kept perfect and true as the pure being of Light that you are." He also told me on the same day, "With the gift of healing comes a great responsibility, but one that is not yours to carry, for the responsibility is Mine." That was a relief—I wouldn't want to carry the responsibility, ever.

So many people ask me if I've ever failed to heal someone. I'll have to repeat this over and over, also. It's not me doing the healings. Of myself, I can do nothing. Nor can you. Unless we surrender our judgments, we're not a clear transparency for God to work through. Man doesn't have the power to heal the mind. That's what I was starting to tell you above, when I was talking about affirming to your subconscious. The mind is above man so something greater than man has to be what heals the mind.

The spirit of Christ/Light/divinity, (whatever you feel comfortable calling It,) is the source of that healing presence. As we saw in the introduction, children don't need any of those words. They open themselves to the Light and just accept it.

As you can see in this room, I don't have a fancy massage table for people to be comfortably worked on. Actually, you're lucky! I just bought a director's chair with the canvas seat and back. Before I got this, you would have had to sit on the floor while I sat behind you. I don't have any fancy gadgets or furniture. What you see is what you get.

One more interruption and, I promise, I'll get on with it. At one of my workshops, my daughter, Jaime, joined me to help in book sales and to answer questions for those who couldn't get to me immediately. She had friends in a nearby town to visit and wanted to take the car to see them. I hesitated because I knew she wasn't going to be back on time. However, I allowed her to go.

She was to be back by 8:00 A.M. the following morning. She didn't arrive, but I had been awake since the early hours and knew she wouldn't. At first, I was starting to get tense because, within the car was this chair that I use, my tape player, music, books, flyers, everything I was going to need throughout the day. People were depending on me and I was going to arrive nakedly alone, with just the presence of God.

When I realized that, I thought, Well, by damn, that's going to have to be enough! If Jaime gets back before I actually leave, that's okay and if not, that's okay, too. Peace be with me! I surrendered the judgments that it was bad that Jaime wasn't back on time, and I surrendered the human judgments that it would be good if she did get back on time. I was truly at peace and beyond that, nothing else mattered. Jaime arrived three minutes before I walked out the door.

And so you have it. Right? If you have peace of mind, you've got God and you've got it all, right? (You'd better pay attention. I'm going to test you on this later! Or, life will!)

All right, sit in this canvas chair and get comfortable. The reason I bought a canvas chair is because I am able to reach any part of your body without asking you to stand up, roll over, or turn. I am able to energy sense a body for hot and cold spots, and you will learn this, too.

I'm going to turn on some very pretty and relaxing music. I, personally, don't need that stimulation. I've been doing this for so long and have such a developed sense of concentration that I can do it while the kids are fighting, while cartoons are blaring, or as you remember, standing outside a restaurant in the light of day.

Once I lay my hands on a person's head, some people go to sleep and others start crying. They say they feel the love so strongly. Please, just relax. Cross or uncross your legs, whichever is most comfortable for you. Take a long, slow deep breath, close your eyes and just listen to the music. You may begin to see pinpoints of white Light or other colors within your mind's eye. For this time we have together, I want you to feel like you're the most important person in my entire life. Because, in this moment, you are.

CHAPTER 13

I'm not here to save the world,
I'm here spending my time and energy
trying to make it a nicer place to be

As I'm standing behind you, I'm sure you can hear my two hands rubbing against one another. This is turning on the electricity so it can flow. For the next forty minutes, I'm not going to talk (unless divinely guided to do so.) You want a miracle? Let's start with that one, Gloria *not* talking! (Months ago, in our bedroom, I yawned really, really big. I said to Kirk, "Wow, I'll bet it got dark in here, huh?" He laughed and said, "No . . . but it sure got quiet for a minute!")

This will sound shocking, but I'm not here, during this life, to heal people's lives. God asked me to spiritually awaken His children from their past slumber of negative beliefs and fears, as well as to heal the minds of mankind. I'm not supposed to focus on their pains or illnesses or I would spend a life doing so. My service is to activate their spiritual centers so that each person is connected to their source.

If, in helping you get a jump start, and you receive a miracle in the process, then we'll give thanks. But, please understand that it is not a miracle that we are seeking by making that connection to the source. (Or, at least we shouldn't be.) We are seeking for the shift in awareness and, once we have that, the healing occurs.

I'm going to send photos, featuring my daughter Danielle as an

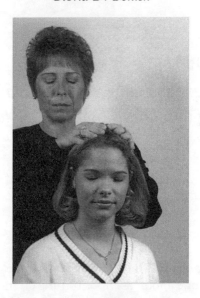

Photo 1 shows the balancing of the left and right brain hemisphere. When this area is balanced, your creativity flows. If this area is closed, you are living life the hard human way, relying on a separateness, and handling life on your own. Your life is God's business. If you take care of His, He will take care of yours.

example, home with you. She is, of course, the one who taught me how "to give others a little extra love."

The photographs will show you where and how to lay hands on yourself or another person. Along with the pictures, I'll provide a short description of why you're laying-on-of-hands in these positions and what it's doing. (The human mind likes to be intellectually stimulated and think it's doing something and playing a part in all this. In the beginning, this is great, but as you grow in awareness, you'll find yourself totally depending upon the source/inner voice/telepathy/intuition.)

With my hands briskly rubbed, I'm placing them on top of your head. This is the left and right brain hemisphere.

Briskly rub your palms together. (This turns on the electricity/energy/love so that it can flow through you.) Laying hands on this area balances the energy fields, allowing you to tap into the creative side within you. It also helps you to have one foot in the spiritual world and one foot in the physical world. Many people in mental institutions, through drugs or other means, have whacked out and are hearing voices. They are carrying on conversations with people others can't see and it's because this area isn't balanced. The drugs may quiet the voices, but they won't cure the consciousness that created it. Hearing the still, small voice within us is different than talking to dead people, those dear departed in other dimensions. Also, those who hear the voices have torn the veil that separates the fourth (and other) dimensions from the physical world. Don't be scared! By laying hands on the left and right brain hemisphere, and seeking the Light, you will heal and seal the injury.

(Having this area balanced also means that you can see and hear spirit and/or ascended masters. After the chat, you should go clean the bathroom or mop a floor. Balance!)

The veil and the spiritual body can be healed and sealed, which will bring those who are too far out back in. For those who are spiritually on the path, they find themselves hungering and thirsting for all the books they can consume and all the knowledge they can feed into their minds. At times, not being aware of discerning information and people's suggestions (or channelings) they go too far overboard and learn a lesson.

Placing the hands on the left and right brain hemisphere, allows the person to open spiritually to the creative world, without losing the connection and logic with the physical world. Logic and ego, by the way, are gifts. Don't minimize their effectiveness and importance unless you, at this very moment, are able to walk through walls or on water.

You might notice, as your hands are in the position on top of the left and right brain hemisphere, with your eyes closed, that all you can see is black. Waves of black, perhaps. Black is not bad, so do not be frightened or think that you're not able to do this. Black is the mass consciousness, which teaches all of us, as we are born into this world, that there are two powers: one evil, one good. This consciousness promotes the idea that there is a power in opposition to God. Black is pain and black can also be fear. Again, don't be frightened or feel inferior to my present capabilities. Silently, ask for peace.

(If you are laying hands on yourself or another and several minutes pass and you continue to only see darkness, lean your head as far back as you can, as if you are looking at the ceiling. With your eyes still closed, use your inner vision by rolling your eyes back, almost as if you were trying to look out through the top of your head. This position lifts the veil that separates the physical and spiritual consciousness so that the Light can flow into your mind.)

Night is black, but a streetlight or a light turned on within a home consumes the darkness. The spiritual light within does the same thing. In the beginning, God created the world and in doing so, He said, "Let there be Light!" As you close your eyes, you can ask for the same thing if all you see within your spiritual vision is darkness.

As I lay hands on people, all I ever ask is this: "God, I am here. Peace be with me." I ask for nothing more, but I'll settle for nothing less. You, as a healer for yourself or another, must come to a peaceful state of mind, without prejudgments of the human appearance or you are not effective. This means that whatever you are looking at, you must surrender the human judgment. If it's a child, you must be able to state with authority, "If this child lives, that's okay, if this child dies, that's okay too. Peace be with me!"

Well, any person in their right mind can't say that, because, dang it, does matter if the child dies. I know this and you know this, but if you continue to have human judgments that it's "good" if the child lives and "bad" if the child dies, you are continuing to live within the dual world of beliefs. There are no opposing powers, except in the conditioned minds of mankind. Under God's law, there isn't a bad power (like Satan) to be beaten up or overcome by God's power.

Also, I'm stating this again, and if I repeat myself a bazillion times throughout this day, you must understand: We are not asking God to heal a disease or mend a broken heart or to do anything for us. The reason why we can't and should never try to use God for our own human needs or selfish purposes will be explained in more detail later.

Living, or attempting to heal under duality, will get you nowhere. You must arrive at a neutral/peaceful state of mind for spirit to work through you. God has no judgments of the human scene as we've all been taught. He only knows us, as Himself, created in His image which is Light. Any other appearance is a reflection. Illness, lack, and fear are mesmerizing, hypnotic human suggestions. He asked me to awaken you from the trance. Are you ready? I'll count to three and when I do, you will remember that what I'm saying is true and that you're already aware of it, but had only forgotten. One . . . two . . . three . . .

As an instrument, whether your inner vision is black or not, you ask for peace. If you're scared of the situation, the possible fearful outcome in the human scene or appearance, continue to keep your eyes closed and silently chant, "Peace, peace, peace be with me." Or, quietly and silently ask only for the presence of God. Keep your attention focused on only wanting to see a pinpoint of white light in your inner vision, and ask for peace or the presence, which are actually the same thing: one is a feeling, and the other is visual.

Remember, there is no power for good or bad in the appearance or situation. By surrendering that human judgment of two powers in opposition, you have opened your mind to be used as the instrument for God's grace. You will meet human judgments of "good and bad" throughout every day for the rest of your life. This service and healing begins this moment and continues moment to moment. Every person in the world has the power within them to heal their lives. Five percent of the masses has the power and ability to heal the multitudes. In order for me to effectively heal the masses of people, it takes a twenty-four-hour devotion and dedication on a conscious, unconscious, and superconscious level. For you, personally, it takes only the willingness to heal your fears and the fears of those you meet.

With your eyes closed, after a few moments or minutes, you may begin to see a tiny pinpoint of white light in the center of your inner vision. (The pinpoints of light look almost like a Christmas tree light flickering.) If you are so fortunate to see this, wonderful. If not, that's okay, too. If you do, the mind has just opened to

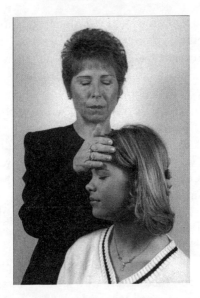

Photo 2 shows the position to balance the pineal and pituitary (master) gland. If these areas are not balanced, it will be difficult to make a decision or have enough energy to maintain your physical body. Balancing these areas produces clarity of thought and accelerated healing and gives you added Light to carry for others.

receive the Light. You may also see a violet Light or other colors, in splotches. If you do, it's all right, and if you don't, that's all right, too. With continued practice, you will.

The violet Light of which I speak is the activity of spirit within my consciousness. Other terms may be the healing Light, the Holy Spirit, the violet transmuting flame, etc. This Light is the source that dissolves the black (fear, error, or pain) within the human mind/consciousness. The violet Light purifies the consciousness so that the perfection, which God has already created, can shine through and manifest into the physical form.

There. I've taught you how to be a healer or how to open yourself to be used as a healing instrument. If you closed this book now, in reality, I would have told all you will ever need to know. Since I love to talk, however, I'm going to keep sharing the understanding I've been given.

I'm going to move my hands now so that the right palm goes over the front of the forehead and the left hand rests at the base of the head.

Rub your palms together briskly. Place the right palm on the forehead and the left hand on the back of the head. This position balances the pineal and pituitary glands. If the forehead is hot, this usually tells me that the person has a headache, stress, and/or high blood pressure. It also tells me that the "third eye" or spiritual vision is closed: you are having a hard time making a decision or are afraid of the choices, the fear that you'll make the wrong choice. If this is going on in your world, it should be the first clue that the third eye is closed. Whenever this occurs, throughout your day, rub your hands and immediately lay hands on this area, closing your eyes and asking for peace.

If you're having a hard time making a decision and discover that the third eye is closed, don't be frightened that you won't be able to open it (since you're just a beginner at this). Fear, doubt, and confusion aren't "bad," they are tools to give you awareness that you have blocked the flow of energy, disconnecting from the source that continually gives unless you block it. You will feel immediate results as it opens (usually is within five-to-ten minutes, but it actually can be sooner). Your thoughts will be clearer. You will feel lighter. You will have immediate feedback. Healing isn't hard, and if anyone tells you otherwise, they want your power. They want you to depend on them. I want you to know the truth (of one power) and I want you to depend only on God.

The third eye is the imagination. Remember? We're made in God's image? We're in God's imagination, held within the mind of God. Our imagination or imaging ability is our link within that mind. Here's a simple exercise: With your eyes open or closed, can you imagine a red apple? Can you see the brown stem and the two green leaves attached to the stem? Can you see the dewdrop of moisture on the apple? If you can see those things, your third eye is open. If you can't imagine it or other events and their outcome, the third eye is closed. Rub your hands together and lay them on the forehead and the back of the head now.

If you can see it, within your mind, it already is. This one-liner should bring you the deepest peace that you have ever known. (Not the peace that is opposite war, but the peace that passeth all human understanding.) There's no power for good or bad in the human judgments of two opposing forces. We surrender those judgments and allow the peace and grace of God to descend through our heightened sense of awareness to manifest in our physical world. When the human mind is silent from the judgments of two powers, the reality of God's presence flows through our minds and manifests as perfection.

Years ago, a dear friend of mine was afraid to leave her home. She was frightened and phobic of anything that extended beyond her driveway. She and her husband had purchased a summer home, years before, but now they were unable to use it. One afternoon, I asked her, "Can you see yourself arriving at the summer home and unpacking the car?" She replied, "Yes." I offered, "If you can see yourself doing that, you have already arrived safely." I questioned again, "Can you see yourself arriving back home and unpacking the vehicle, having enjoyed your vacation?" Once again, she said, "Yes."

Though this may seem too easy or even trivial, it is, in fact, our spiritual vision going before us to prepare our way. I explained to my friend that if she could see a safe arrival, in both directions, she could get into the vehicle without fear. If there ever came a time that she couldn't see herself arriving safely, she shouldn't go until she closed her eyes, asked for peace, and allowed that violet Light to purify the consciousness and prepare the outer perfection.

I use this gift with all my kids and family members. If they ask to go to the movies in a nearby city and I can see them arriving safely, there and back home, they are allowed to go. If there is ever a time that I can't see the end result, they will remain at home.

I use this gift every day. It's imagination, but that word minimizes the usefulness of the gift. You can also call it clairvoyance, but it means the same. It's spiritual vision, plain and simple. We all have it, it's not something given only to a gifted few. Just not all of us trust it, yet.

My answering machine used to say, "You can call me opti-mystic, you can call me psychic, or you can call me again because I'm positive, I'm not here right now!" People of a religious back-ground get the heebie-jeebies whenever they hear the word "psy-chic" and automatically refer to it as "of the Devil." We've now learned that the devil is just the belief that there's a power in op-position to God, the human judgments of good and bad. We sur-render the human judgment. There is no power for good or bad in clairvoyance, psychic gifts, or spiritual vision, for God is all that is. My consciousness of God appears as my vision. There is no separa-tion between God and my vision.

When the third eye is balanced again, you will know it. You will have opened the imagination channel and you will see what's before you. (Trusting it is another thing. We'll get to that later.)

Don't be surprised or frightened if, while your eyes are closed, your inner vision opens to what appears as a widescreen TV, and you receive inspiration directly. This is what occurs when divine beings or other beings of Light come to me to inspire me with awareness of my gifts. I swear, I don't know why anyone on this planet uses drugs, because revelations and visions are a natural high. You will know such sweet, sweet bliss as you open yourself to that inner power. The opening of the third eye is the beginning of spiritual awakening and you will be shown all that you are to do.

Many times, in my meetings with people, they ask if I ever see "my Boss" manifest in the physical dimension and if so, how He appears. The answer is, "Yes, He has appeared many times in the physical world to me." You're aware of the heat vibrational waves off hot pavement in the summer, right? Well, when He slows His vibratory rate, this is the appearance I see with my physical eyes. Where His head is, golden sparks radiate from Him. I can see Him and His entire energy field.

Back to teaching: the right hand is on the third eye while the left hand has been resting on the back of the head. The left hand is activating the pineal gland, the seat to the soul. When the pineal gland is empowered and balanced, all the other glands are acti-vated. The pineal is the master gland (the boss of the body). If it is imbalanced, you are not receiving enough electricity/Light to feed your physical body.

The left hand, on the base of the head, is rebalancing this area. With your eyes closed and looking for the inner pinpoint of Light or the violet Light (and asking only for peace), you will begin to feel an extreme sense of warmth flowing throughout your body. Placing your hand on this area and activating this spiritual center allows the body to be filled with all the energy/Light/electricity you will need daily, but also allows you to be given the amount of Light that you will carry so that others who reach out to you do not take from the energy you need to individually maintain health.

How many of us are codependents? Be honest, raise your hand. We will give every last ounce of energy to help another, but aren't quite as loving to ourselves. If you want to remain codependent, that's okay (and if not, that's okay, too) but if you want to continue to share, then at least tap into the divine source so that you don't feel so hammered when you've given too much of yourself.

To all you ladies and gentlemen: when you've been to a beauty shop and you've had your hair done, have you ever noticed, either on that same day or the following day, that the lower part of your head is sore? It's because the pineal gland has been closed, at least to some degree, and it has created physical pain because it's not al-lowing as much electricity to flow as it should. Rub your hands and place them on this area immediately. Open yourself to the divine power so that you are being spiritually fed all that you need (with-out taking from another). Get it direct.

In this stressful world in which we all live, there is no way to get the amount of rest or eat as much as we need to restore our bodies. We need to spiritually awaken and get the energy direct. Many suf-fer from obesity, which makes it appear that they are pretty well fed, when in fact, they are probably the ones who are starving the most for love. Surrender your human judgments (personally or to-ward others) and hug a fat person today.

I like to use this example: The human body is a "shell" for the Light within. Shell is also a gas station where you drive your phys-

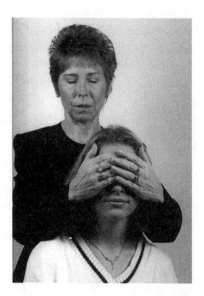

Photo 3 shows the student how to raise our energy level quickly, without needing a nap or full night's rest. This position also should be done daily to keep the mind's eye open.

ical vehicle to if you need more energy. You put the nozzle into the gas tank, connecting to an unseen tank beneath the ground. You can't see the gasoline, but you know it's there, because the needle on your car rises to the full mark. You can't see God's energy (unless you close your eyes and see the violet Light flooding into your inner vision), but you know it's there because you will be able to feel the difference. Humans say, "I'll believe it when I see it!" Well, alrighty then—close your eyes and see the Light. See the difference it makes in your life when you stop trying to live your life the human/hard way, usually "going without," and open yourself to the source within that knows that you need to eat, knows you need clothing, a roof, and to be well maintained in this third dimension we all term "reality." Go within or go without.

Standing behind you, I'm going to place my right hand over your right eye and my left hand over your left eye.

Briskly rub your palms together and place them over your eyes. I do this before I get out of bed. No one would need glasses or corrective eyewear if they did this every day. Stresses of the day deplete the energy of the eyes and laying hands on them feeds them the electricity and balance they need. This position keeps the third eye open. By placing your hands on the back of the head, you will have activated the two prime spiritual centers. This position also, throughout the day or evening, serves as a quick pick-me-up energy boost without a nap or full night's sleep.

I have knowingness within me as to how long I should keep my hands in each position. So will you. It may be a few moments, it may be ten minutes. If your temples are hot, you may be under stress or have high blood pressure. Here's what to do:

Slowly move your hands from the eyes to the temples. Place your right hand over the right temple and the left hand over the left temple. Once the temples feel cool, you'll know that the blood pressure has returned to normal, and you'll be feeling calmer.

You have an inner teacher who may have you do things differently, so be open, be receptive, don't think that you must do it the way Gloria taught or that it's not going to work. Hardly. I'm giving you a guideline, but you will learn to intuitively listen to and trust your inner voice, guiding you each step of the way, through thought. You may be told, after balancing the left and right brain hemisphere, to place one hand on a knee and the other on the toe. You will be guided where to place your hands and you will also know when the sharing of energy is complete.

If you, in the beginning, don't have confidence, that's okay, too. I didn't either. Remember, however, that it's not you (the human personality) who's doing anything. You are merely the instrument. It is your individual consciousness of God that is doing the greater work. As each human judgment is surrendered and healed, the purification of your consciousness occurs, and this is the healing agent. (You, the personality, don't have the power to screw things up, okay?)

From the eyes (or the temples), I move my hands down so that the left hand is on the person's left ear and the right hand is on their right ear.

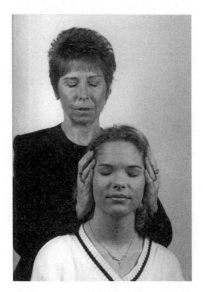

Photo 4 illustrates the hand positions that balance and bring forth the power of clairaudience. If balanced, you will hear a still, small voice within—the voice of your soul.

Briskly rub your palms together and place them on your ears. Whew! This is another important spiritual center and one that I spend more time on than even a place where someone may believe they have cancer, a tumor, or something serious.

Clairaudience (or the ability to spiritually "hear" Divine Guidance) is a gift, given to everyone (not a select few) that allows us to listen to the voice within and receive the guidance concerning the part we play in the divine plan. If the ears are in balance, our gift of clairaudience is turned on and activated and we will hear everything we need to know. It may whisper to purchase a book or see a physician or a spiritual healer, which will heal the consciousness. Who knows what you will be told, but this center is most important. I will explain later, in more detail, what it means if your ears ring.

From the ears, I move my hands briefly to the jaw areas.

Briskly rub your palms together and lay them on your jawline.

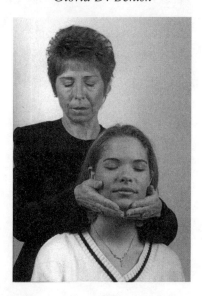

Photo 5 shows how to place your hands to locate hot or cold spots along the jawline. Balancing this area relieves not only sore throats, but grinding teeth, cavities, toothaches, and other head problems.

This isn't activating a spiritual center per say, but on most people I've ever worked on, their jawlines are cold. Like the temples, it's not necessary to do, but just part of the overhaul. When the jawlines are cold, it tells me that the glands aren't getting enough electricity/energy, and the lack of energy is also effecting the gums. (So many have gum disease. Do you see why this area needs to be brought into balance?)

I was sitting in a restaurant one evening, years ago. My friend introduced a man, who joined us at the table. I asked if he'd like to see a menu, and he responded, "No, I have a toothache. I couldn't eat a thing." The man continued to complain of his pain, mentioning that it was Friday and his dentist wouldn't be open until Monday.

I told him that I was a spiritual healer, offering my services. He denied the offer with a bold remark, "I don't believe in that bullshit!" I rubbed my palms together, smiled at him, and replied,

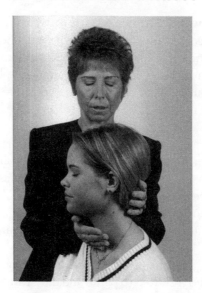

Photo 6 shows the hand positions to balance the thyroid and parathyroid. If you know an AIDS patient, just wait and see what happens when you get your hands on them. The healing of this condition is impressively accelerated.

"Yeah . . . sometimes I don't either, but peace be with you anyway." With those words, I touched my left hand to his cheek for a millisecond, and he looked like I had hit him with a baseball bat. He jumped back in his seat, almost as if he'd been hit by a lightning bolt and exclaimed, "Son of a b, it doesn't hurt anymore!" I replied, "I know."

From the jawline, I move my right hand to the front of the throat and my left hand to the back of the neck.

Briskly rub your palms together and place on the throat and back of the neck. The neck holds tension, and the parathyroid needs to be balanced. When the parathyroid is balanced, it strengthens the immune system. In my experiences with people, the thyroid is the one that I most often feel out of balance. (If the thyroid is cold, it's sluggish and low. If hot, it's over-active.) Don't ask me why, but if these areas are balanced, there wouldn't be an AIDS patient in this world. I'm not a doctor and know nothing about medical terms concerning left and right brain hemisphere, pituitary, pineal gland, thyroid, or parathyroid. All I know is that spirit guides me with these words and tells me one-liners to share. Discern. See your medical doctor as you continue to expand your consciousness. I'm just telling you what has worked for me in healing others.

While I was a guest speaker in prison, an inmate walked up to me, put a note into my hand, and walked away since I had many women lined up for healing hugs. Following the last hug, I opened the note and it read, "My name is Beverly, I'm HIV positive. Please pray for me." Because I was so involved with hugging, I didn't get a chance to look at her face. I would never recognize her among so many people.

Immediately, I started asking those around me if they knew a Beverly. None did. I started to panic and didn't want to miss an opportunity like this. I asked again and again if anyone knew her. This time, Beverly overheard me asking and stepped up to me, formally introducing herself.

The guards were lining the women up to take them back to their cells. I only had minutes to do something. I set her in a chair and stood behind her. I skipped all the steps leading up to this one. Against all prison rules and procedures, I placed my left hand on the back of her neck and my right hand on the front of her throat. I closed my eyes, saw the Light and watched as the violet Light flooded my awareness. I felt a shift. . . . I had done my job. We hugged quickly and gave each other our addresses to follow up and said good-bye.

Since then, Beverly has written me twice. She shares that she's feeling much better, is awaiting tests to validate the healing, is teaching other inmates, and is looking forward to going home to be with her children.

Next comes my favorite position, the activation of the spiritual heart center. As I stand behind you, my arms are reaching to the heart area.

Briskly rub your palms together and lay them on your heart cen-

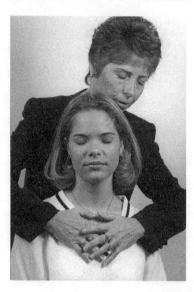

Photo 7 shows the opening and purification of the heart center. When balanced and open, we have self-love and love for all others. If you know any "grumpy Smurfs," or cranky individuals, place your hands in this position and expect a miracle.

ter. Unless you are totally unfeeling, and even if you think you are, I promise you're going to feel extreme warmth coming from my heart center. I'm completely openhearted and all that is being given to me, I'm giving unto you.

This is most generally the moment people start crying (if they didn't when I first touched them). Never have they felt as loved as they do in this moment. Nothing beyond this moment matters. I have my eyes closed and am watching as the violet Light waves and waves, flooding the person and myself with ecstacy.

Anything that happened in the outer world at this moment wouldn't matter. All that matters is this moment. The purification of the heart. The purification of the consciousness that's attracted others to take our feelings and throw them on the floor and stomp and spit on them. (Excuse me, but that's what has happened to 99.9 percent of everyone who's ever lived in this third dimension.)

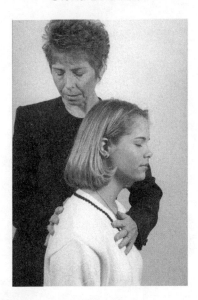

Photo 8 shows you how to massage and "figure eight" the spine, bringing the back into balance and relieving stress and back pain. This procedure also purifies the blood and awakens nerve endings throughout the entire spine.

Pain and fear is dissolved, tears flow, peace is felt, and miracles occur in this moment. Miracles born of love. I'm not speaking of human love, which can be withheld or conditioned, but a supreme divine, unconditional love.

If a person you're working on begins crying or sobbing extremely hard, move your right palm to the forehead and slide your left hand to the solar plexus area. Gentlemen, if you are working on a woman, be cautious, nonsexual and nonthreatening, around a woman's breast area (or she'll probably just slap you into the dirt).

This position softens the emotions and allows a less painful healing to occur.

Place your left hand on the heart center and "figure eight" the spine.

Rub your palms together briskly. Place your left hand on the heart center, and using your right palm, rub your hand in a gentle

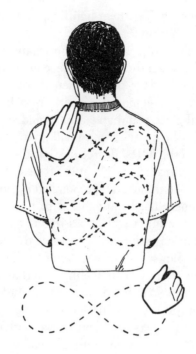

circular/washing motion on the top of the right shoulder and back. Massage the right shoulder, moving in the circular motion. After eight to ten circles on the shoulder, smoothly flow your right hand into a figure-eight pattern, coming to rest on the opposite left shoulder. Use the same massage technique, washing the shoulder area counterclockwise. After eight to ten circles, "figure eight" your hand to a lower section of the back and continue massaging, figure eight back to the left side, and continue down the spine.

I'm calling the motion a figure eight, but it's a horizontal movement across the back. It's actually more like the infinity sign. This motion and exercise balances both sides of the back and also assists in the purification of the blood which runs through the entire spine. It also reawakens the nerve endings to all the major organs.

This is most relaxing and enjoyable. When you have gotten to the bottom of the lower back, using the index and middle fingers of the right hand, gently drag them lightly up the spine. This is also another cleansing motion for the blood.

(This step isn't always necessary, but many times, I've been known to kneel between the legs and place my hands on the stomach, female organs, bladder, pancreas, etc., looking for hot or cold spots/sluggish energy. You may also be drawn to do this, learning to trust that you will place your hands where guided.)

Normally from the heart center, I will go to places where I feel a person's pain. To the fullest degree of what they feel, I feel it. (It definitely gives me incentive to heal it.) If I can feel it, I can heal it. If those who come to me and are numbed by drugs or alcohol, I may overlook something. I must feel it to heal it. So must you.

If we feel what another feels, does this not mean that we are truly one? Pain can travel for miles, entering the hearts and homes of our loved ones. But so can love. If you feel the pain of another, you are not taking it on, you are feeling it so that you can learn to trust where to place your hands in order to heal it. When you channel that Light into your consciousness, the light is dissolving it. Neither you nor the person will walk away with pain. When you can no longer feel it, they won't either, because it's dissolved. No one ends up with the pain. Where darkness once was, the Light has been turned on, the electricity/energy is flowing again and this perfection is reality.

While you're working on another person, if you continue to feel extreme pain, let go and shake the energy from your hands. Before placing your hands back on the person, briskly rub your palms together again. When you're completely finished performing the energy work on another person, wash your hands. Any traces of their energy are cleansed from you. If you continue to feel "echoes of pain" after you've worked on someone, rub your hands together and place them over your eyes for two to ten minutes, or longer. (No one has ever overdosed on love). Keeping your hands over your eyes will "burn off" any remaining negativity or pain. This position also heightens your consciousness and expands your energy field.

I body-scan the person, looking beyond the physical to see the energy fields. I ask the person to stand against a white wall. I look at them for just a few moments and close my eyes. In my inner vision, I can see where the energy isn't moving. I then lay hands on that area and see the white Light, which opens the avenues for the electricity to flow. I recheck them a final time before they leave.

You can do this, also. I know, you think you can't, but you can. You have sat looking out a window at some time or another and closed your eyes. The image of the window is still in your inner vision, isn't it? It's the same with scanning a person's energy field.

Place them against a plain surface, a white wall or outside without anything behind them (because everything has an energy field). Look at them for a few moments, minutes, or hours, if you think you need to. Close your eyes and you will see energies of red, orange, yellow, green, blue, purple, white, and yes, even black. Again, don't let the black scare you. It's just where the energy isn't flowing. Black is blocked energy.

Rub your hands and place them on those spots that are black and watch the energy/Light turn on. It's no longer black (or painful.) It's easy. Red is physical and can be anger. Balance it with the Light. Orange signifies courage. Yellow is emotions and sometimes appears as a mustardy-dirty yellow color. This signifies old, buried emotions. Cleanse the consciousness with the Light. Green is balance and healing. Blue is spiritual (usually to mean that we have angel helpers or Light beings/masters assisting the healing process.) The violet Light is the purification ray, which will dissolve all the misqualified energy. White is the purity of who we truly are, children of God.

In completion, I ask for a heart-to-heart hug as my only payment. All the love that channels through me is not meant for me. It was brought forth into the physical for you. I take nothing that belongs to you because there's plenty for everyone. As I hug you, I place my left hand on your spine and my right hand on the back of your head and request of you, "Don't let go until I tell ya."

I use my left hand to sense the spine for follow-up, to make sure that I don't find any hot or cold spots. Hot just means pain or too much energy; cold means not enough energy. Either one is an imbalance, and when you restore the balance, by laying-on-of-hands and closing your eyes and going into the Light, healing naturally occurs. Nothing mystical or magical, it's just the way it is.

I place my right hand on the back of your head because I'm not going to release you "until I see within my vision a pinpoint of white Light in the center of my vision. Or, until spirit whispers, "It's finished, you can let go now." Sometimes spirit has to say that to me several times because the intense love that is being felt between myself and the person is so incredible, I never want to let go.

I always share this information at workshops, though it doesn't have anything to do with the actual laying-on-of-hands exercises. I believe that anything that can help others, however, is worth sharing. Long ago, I learned this simple procedure and others I have met have also found the information to be useful and valid.

When you get out of bed in the morning and while you're walking to the bathroom, rub your two palms together and place the right hand on the navel. Rub your tummy in a counterclockwise direction from the navel (or just above it), down and to your right, then down to just above the pubic bone, then up and to your left. Imagine a few inches down from your navel, but still above the pubic bone, that there is a number 12, like on a clock. To the left a few inches from the navel, imagine the number 9. A couple inches above the navel, imagine the number 6. Just inches to the right of the navel, imagine the number 3. In the counterclockwise position, rub 12, 9, 6, 3—repeating the entire time on your walk to the bathroom, 12, 9, 6, and 3. Perform this exercise at least twice a day, morning and night.

This exercise relaxes the intestines so you have a comfortable bowel movement. It also helps you lose weight. If you only have one bathroom in your home and find yourself cramping while waiting, if you use this simple exercise, all pain will dissolve. Also, if a baby or small child is constipated, it will ease the gas and distress.

This exercise is also effective if you have the flu and the poop monster hits. It restores the electrical balance and you will be completely surprised at how quickly the painful side effects diminish. I tell people to do this when they first awaken and following their evening meal. This simple knowledge may come in very handy some day.

Okay, I said I wouldn't talk for that hour and I just rambled on and on and on. I would apologize, but you have to admit that you have got to intellectually understand what it is that I do. This is why, when I teach workshops, I will take at least an hour to sit in silence after teaching so that each person present can tap into that stream of energy that I channel into the physical. My greatest work is done in total silence. So is yours.

I'm not here to save the world. Save them from what? I don't believe there's a power in opposition to God. I believe in one power, one presence, one experience. That doesn't mean that I'm sticking my head in the ground, like an ostrich, and being in denial. To the human senses, the world is filled with insanity in various forms. I will surrender those human judgments, one by one until the day I die, and I will watch miracles manifest every moment of my life. I'm one. You're one. We be one (I love to say that!). All right, I'll say it right. We are one. Each one of us who raises our awareness assists in the planetary evolution toward our return to the Garden of Eden, where we will recapture a memory of our innocence, where we will live in peace, by the grace of God.

It's a big job, but someone's gotta do it. I'm going to spend my time and energy making this world a nicer place to be. I don't use God. God uses me. We've been taught to pray to a God and when our prayers are not answered, we believe that it's because He didn't hear us, we're not worthy of a miracle, or that we didn't ask right.

God has given us everything already, it's embodied within our consciousness. We are the ones. Not through prayer, but through opening ourselves, we can allow that greater good within us, to flow into the outer world of form. Close your eyes, open your mind. Go within and watch your outer world transform. It's not my life and your life, our life is one with God. God is life, in every single form. God is the consciousness that animates and demonstrates itself as miracles. You, my friend, are the greatest miracle of all.

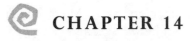

CHAPTER 14
Benish Law

As you're sitting there, relaxing, I'm going to go check on the kids and see if they're enjoying their movie and not having a food fight with the popcorn and treats. I'll be right back.

They're acting like ladies and a gentleman. I do believe in miracles. Again, while you're sitting there and enjoying the moment, I'd like to share a few stories with you to bring my kids and home life into perspective.

One afternoon when D.W. was four years old and Danielle was two, she was standing in front of a drawer in our kitchen. D.W. walked into the room and, in a very mannerly voice, asked her to please move so he could get into the drawer, which held pencils and other miscellaneous junk. In fact, he said it just like this, "Excuse me, Danielle, but I need to get a pencil out of that drawer."

Well, I had to leave the kitchen and look up at the heavens, and that is the first time I ever said, "I do believe in miracles!" You see, normally he would have said, "Get out of the way, stupid, or I'll sock you in the stomach!" (It was my first indication that my meditations and quiet time in the Light were affecting my outer world.)

D.W. was about eight years old, when one day as he got ready for school, he joined me in the kitchen and said, "Mom, I don't want to go to school today." I asked if he was sick and he replied, "No." I questioned, "Is your homework not complete or is someone or something about school bothering you?" Once again, he answered, "No."

Realizing that there wasn't a reason for him to miss school, I said, "D.W., you have to go to school, it's the law." He questioned, "Benish law?" I laughed and said, "No, state and federal!"

I'm going to get up on my soapbox now. Not to preach, but so that we can see eye to eye on what I'm going to explain to you. Man, at his present state of awareness lives under karmic law. Karmic law is the law of cause and effect. Other ways it's referred to are "What you think, you get," "What you sow, you reap," "What goes around, comes around." It's under karmic law that we attract what we love, hate, and fear.

Karmic law is the law of duality, opposing powers of good and evil, a mass conscious belief that we all agree to live under when we incarnate in this third dimension. As simply as I can say it, it all began with Adam and Eve in the Garden of Eden. Eden was heaven (the state of spiritual consciousness), where everything man would ever need appeared, without taking thought.

When Adam and Eve were tempted to eat of the Tree of Knowledge (of Good and Bad), they assumed a role apart from God, becoming dual-minded, and thereafter had to think for themselves and toil by the sweat of their brow to acquire all their needs. It was in the Garden of Eden where the belief that we are separate and apart from God originated.

When Moses had his illumination, he was given the Ten Commandments, which he was to give to the people. The Commandments afforded humankind a guideline to live by if they wanted to continue to live with the belief in two powers. With these "laws," however, humanity could only hope to live a humanly good life.

I have a story that I wrote long ago, which was inspired, I'm sure, by spirit. I can't remember it by heart, but it went something like this:

Moses was a dreamer and spent his days lying around and looking into the sky, watching the clouds. His greatest desire was to know God, and those around him scorned and ridiculed him for his nonsensical ways. He was a joke to all those who toiled throughout the days to maintain their lives and families.

Though he was ridiculed, he continued to meditate and contemplate God, wanting only to know God personally. He wanted nothing that the physical world had to offer. His desire paid off, when one afternoon, he heard the Voice of God calling him to the Mount of Transfiguration.

Moses climbed, day after day, higher and higher up the side of the mountain. Each step was harder than the last, but he knew he must persevere. Time held no more meaning for him and if it took years to reach that heightened sense of awareness and come face to face with God, then so be it.

At last, he arrived at the peak of the mountain, where he had heard God speak. God, at that moment, asked Moses to take the Commandments back to his people and burned the messages into slabs of stone. God gave something physical for all the world to see.

On the way down the mountain, Moses tripped and fell and the tablet rolled end over end, tumbling down the steep mountain and, as it came to rest, the tablets were broken into countless pieces. Moses was saddened and frustrated. He had two choices: he could go to the people who mocked him and explain that he had been given the tablets containing God's Commandments and explain his accident, or he could go back up the mountain and have God engrave another set.

Knowing the awareness of the people, he knew that if he took only the Word of God to the people, he would continue to be mocked and ridiculed. They couldn't understand his hunger for spiritual awakening, how could they understand something they couldn't see?

With a heavy sigh, Moses reclimbed the Mount of Transfiguration and came face to face with the Creator once again, requesting a second set of the "laws" for the people to live by, with, and under. He returned to the masses and was ridiculed and mocked anyway.

The moral of this story is twofold. One, I hope you understand that the Commandments were "broken" long before we ever got them and, two, cast not your pearls before swine. Before you take offense or think I've just gone into judgment calling unenlightened souls little piglets, please understand that it is meant in its biblical sense that, under karmic law, has proven itself as a fact. In my earlier years of attempting to share with those who could not yet understand, I received adversity and many hard feelings.

I'm teaching you to discern whom you share with (in the beginning), as well as when to speak and when to remain silent. Until you feel you can speak with authority and without attempting to defend the truth, never attempt to share your spiritual understanding or experiences unless first asked or unless, through knowingness, it's appropriate. (It will help you avoid adversity.) It is not our job to force our beliefs on others, expecting them to reach new levels of awareness. The greatest teachings are done through demonstration and allowing others to seek us.

Everything I write and share can only come from experience, not from something I've read or been told, because God is a personal experience, not an intellectual philosophy.

On October 5, 1985, my thirty-second birthday, I awoke and spirit whispered that I was going to have a Oneness Ceremony later that evening. I was told if I drank alcohol while out at my birthday dinner, the ceremony would be delayed. Not denied, just delayed (because alcohol, under karmic law, along with my judgments against it, was going to lower my vibration and awareness).

I had no idea what a Oneness Ceremony was, nor did any of the friends I shared this information with throughout the day. However, after my friends departed from my birthday celebration, I went to lay down in D.W.'s room. (He had cuddled with his dad in the master bedroom) and since I didn't know what this meditation would bring, I found sanctity in my son's bedroom.

When the divine presence comes to me (I see Him with my eyes open), or comes to my awareness (I see Him with my eyes closed), it's never with a lot of fanfare or trying. I just relax and He appears. On this evening, after I laid down, I closed my eyes and immediately, I saw a pinpoint of white Light in my inner vision.

The Light got bigger and bigger and, out of the Light, stepped Jesus. He began walking toward me.

As he got within inches of me, I looked up into his eyes, which held only love. He asked, "Do you give yourself to Me?" With no forethought or afterthought, I replied, "Totally, without doubt," not realizing consciously what was being asked of me.

He bent down and kissed my cheek and placed his arms around me for a heart-to-heart hug and I watched as two souls melded into one. All of "Gloria" disappeared, as did His individual personality, and we became one in the Light.

He asked me six times to open my eyes, but I couldn't. I was paralyzed by fear, for the entire house had started breathing. It felt as though the home was reverberating, and it was frightening me. Liquid fire flowed throughout my veins which didn't seem to ease my fears. A seventh time, He said, "Absolve your fears and know that you are in My hands . . . and that no harm can ever touch you." He continued, "I am breathing life into you."

At that moment, I opened my eyes and, in a completely darkened room, I could see myself as total white Light. Light was coming out of every single cell, fiber, muscle, tissue, and organ of my being. I was a glow-in-the-dark-Gloria. The "breathing" stopped as He said, "I will always be with you."

Afterward, I lay in the darkness, my mind spinning, wanting to memorize every moment of the experience. But at the same time, I knew I would never forget. I had felt the deepest level of love ever possible. I had met the Creator face to face, and the memory of it all was burned into my soul forever.

A baptism of fire had occurred. In the Bible, it says that the first cleansing of the planet would be with water. Thus, Noah and his story unfolded. The second cleansing, promised within the pages of the Bible, is to be with fire. Do not be frightened that our planet will burn with fire or nuclear warfare. It is the spiritual awakening and baptism of fire (done within your individual consciousness) with the unconditional pure love, which feels like fire throughout your veins. It is the awakening of the divine consciousness that lies dormant within you. It is the rebirth that religions speak of.

In that Ceremony of Oneness, I felt as if I had died, and I didn't really want to come back into this physical world. But my "Boss" said I had to come back, because I had "service to perform in His Name." (Bummer.) I also felt as if I had united, almost in a marriage ceremony, with Christ, and was reborn of divine love. There you have it: death, birth, and marriage. They always seem to travel in threes, don't they?

You may wonder why I wouldn't share this supernatural, sensational event in the first chapter of a book? Why would I wait until chapter 14 to reveal it?

When I first spiritually awakened, I shared my experience with others. Some of them were envious. After all, there are so many people trying to connect to that source, and here I had had the experience with no effort and without seeking.

Others tried to convince me I "had gone overboard." Many began looking to me as if I were some "great white guru!" I never boasted about it, I simply shared the experience in the hope that I could prepare others for a similar experience. My Oneness Ceremony was important because it connected me to my source.

It is important for you to know that none of us should try to prepare for this experience. If it hasn't yet happened for you, it's not because you haven't ommmed or chanted enough. It's not because you're not using enough crystals or even praying right. God calls us, we don't call Him. We open ourselves to Him, through closing our eyes and going within. He does the rest. If you haven't had miracles or spiritual experiences, it's not because you don't deserve them or because you are a bad person. Your calling will come, at the perfect time, so be at peace.

And, when it does, if you hear the breath of the Holy Spirit aloud or feel liquid fire in your veins, don't be afraid. You're safe, you're loved (more than you can consciously accept at this moment in time). Again, be at peace. Allow my experience to serve you in your acceptance of Oneness.

Oneness. The word, in the spiritual world of our physical planet, rings like poetry. It means nothing, however, unless you understand all that that simple word means. It means what it says. We are one in the mind of God. There aren't two minds, His and ours. There is one mind. (Our individual aspect of that mind, however, is clouded with beliefs in dual powers needing to battle things out, and the winner gets our soul. Hogwash! Oops, there's that "swine" word again.)

We are individual aspects and expressions of God's mind. We have made ourselves separate and apart from that greater good, thinking we have to do things on our own. Oneness means that God isn't going to reward and punish. Punishment is what we get when we think we're bad or we aren't in harmony with others or ourselves. Reward is what comes naturally when you (re)capture a memory of your oneness with God.

God isn't health and disease. He doesn't punish people with disease if they think negative thoughts. Thought has no power, unless living under karmic law and mentally manipulating that realm of consciousness. God *is* health.

It isn't bad if we don't have money and good if we do. Money, of itself has no power for good or bad. When you surrender this and every human judgment of good and bad, you're back in Eden, you're back at peace with yourself and God.

To overcome living under karmic law, or being subjected to the laws of weather and disease, you must come to a peaceful state of mind. Remove your judgment that there are two powers in opposition. You meet every appearance in the outer world and dissolve the judgments as they appear to you. You surrender the judgment, you become a master of your life, and you live in peace.

I live under spiritual law, God's law, by grace (experiencing life as one power, one presence, one experience, of good). God is life. He is my life, your life—the life of all that is. We don't have separate lives, we are one and this is why I'm able to heal over long distances. Distance is a man-made concept. Consciousness (which you and me truly are) is unlimited, pure, and infinite.

Benish law is having to make your bed before school, do your homework before you watch TV, eat your vegetables, don't weight-lift your sister and then hammer her head into the ground, no fighting, no biting, no scratching, no kicking. Get the point?

Karmic law is living with negatives and extremes. Today health, tomorrow illness; today wealth and plenty, tomorrow, lack. Karmic law is mass consciousness that means that bad things happen to good people (even those who live by the Commandments). It's being under the influence of insanity and false teachings of two powers.

God's law is oneness. No longer fluctuating between the good and bad because God is only good. Living under spiritual law, you no longer have to take thought for what you will eat, wear, or do. The grace of God lives through you and as you. It is peace on earth, good will toward man. It is our return to Eden.

CHAPTER 15

$2 + 2 = 4$

*It's all adding up, one can easily see,
perfection already exists in spiritual reality*

Please join me in the kitchen while I stir the steak stew in the crockpot, and as I sort out the piles of the kids' laundry, (which will probably end up on the floor, under their beds, or tucked in the closet instead of in their drawers). Sometimes they try their darndest to push my buttons, ya know what I mean?

Please, just follow me around the house for a few minutes and I'll share another story or two that I feel is important for your awareness. When I first began having such incredible experiences, I turned to friends and books for answers. I remember one book, in particular, that guided me to surround and protect myself (and home) with God's golden white Light. Since I didn't know what I was doing and all of this was scary (and exciting), you can bet that I was surrounding myself all day long with golden white Light.

At the time of this incident, I was living in Sacramento. I had a dream and, in the dream, my family was being burglarized. The "bad guys" came in through the side garage door, in the dream, and wiped us out. In the dream, I headed to the telephone and I kept thinking, "Dial 911," but I seemed to be paralyzed with fear.

In reality, there had been a rash of burglaries in our neighborhood and I was feared being vulnerable. (Under karmic law, we attract what we love, hate, and fear, remember?) When I had the dream, I began sharing it with friends and family. Was the dream literal or symbolic, I questioned. I got more frightened and then my nightly prayers began begging for God's golden white Light to surround and protect our home, and then I also added—from the burglars.

In the dream, I was also forewarned that we would be hit a second time "because I was such an easy mark."

The dream was a precognitive warning. We were burglarized. They came through the side door of our garage, as I was shown. They opened the garage door and because my husband was such a neat-nik and all the tools were in original boxes and neatly stacked on the shelves, the burglars walked away with thousands of dollars of uninsured tools. The second time we were burglarized, they took every riding toy my children owned from our backyard.

I questioned everyone, "What did I do wrong? What did I do to attract this?" Because whatever it was, I certainly didn't want to ever do it again. No one could give me the answers I sought. I felt frustrated. The books couldn't tell me. I finally had to go within and receive the awareness directly.

I created the burglars. I created the power in opposition to God! (I also learned that to see a telephone in a dream is a message and to pay attention!)

Each night I was asking for protection "from the burglars." There were no burglars, until I created them within my consciousness. To make this clearer, perhaps this is another good example for you to see what I'm saying: If you believe that there are drunk drivers (or buttheads) on the highway, you are creating the situation, and you will attract one of those drunk drivers/buttheads through your judgment that it's bad to drink and drive. (Which it is under karmic law, but to rise above the experiences of the pairs of opposites, we must surrender judgment.)

Instead, affirm that the divine intelligence governs all those on the roadway. God is driving those vehicles. Through your awareness and acceptance of one power, you'll be used as an instrument to help others remain safe. Do not create a power in opposition to God, nor the separation that you are divinely protected, but that the drunk drivers/buttheads aren't. God isn't a respecter of any person or sect. He pours out His goodness to everyone.

Heal your human judgments. As each judgment appears, dissolve it with Light, asking for divine peace. Trust me, the judgments appear in countless ways in all our days!

I'm telling you, I still have the judgments, also. I am not self-righteous, trying to convince everyone that I'm perfect, because it just wouldn't be true. (I probably work harder than anyone I know, attempting to dissolve each judgment as it appears so that I can be a more capable and pure channel for the healings to occur through.) I'm all-knowing, however, not a know-it-all. I'm doing the best I can with the awareness I have.

Hopefully, with that preparation and explanation, you won't think I'm a total butthead when I tell you what I did—years ago, okay? But, not to mean that it might not ever happen again, also.

The story unfolds with sharing that I was close friends with a woman whose two children played daily in my home. I had these extras on a constant basis and was never paid for my services of baby-sitting. (Not that I was asking for financial reimbursement, I just thought it was what a friend was supposed to do.)

When my children were toddlers, I found myself needing a sitter and called upon the friend to watch my children for an afternoon. Without hesitation, she said, "No." I was hurt, but I think I was more angry than I was hurt. I never asked anyone to watch my children, and this was an important appointment I could not miss.

I called a stranger across the street and she, without hesitation, agreed to keep my children for the few hours. I no sooner hung up, when my first friend called and requested a healing. Though she had just denied me of her services, I pretended to be nice on the telephone. After I hung up and as I was walking away from the call, my inner angry thoughts said, It will be a cold day in Hell before I heal her, when she wouldn't even baby-sit for me! (Heavy sigh. And I meant it.)

Without judgment, my inner voice said, "Gloria, you do not have the right to say who does or doesn't receive healings." Without question or argument, knowing my conscience/still, small voice was right, I sat in the recliner, kicked back, closed my eyes, went into the Light, felt the inner shift, and knew my friend was healed.

The telephone rang immediately and she said, "Thanks, I got the healing! Do you still need the baby-sitter?"

Amazing, isn't it? I didn't see the whole picture. When my friend first refused to sit for the children for me, I didn't know she was sick. How many times have situations occurred in our lives and we don't have the entire picture and assume that people have reacted certain ways for various reasons, when perhaps we didn't truly know what was going on behind the scenes?

You're probably wondering where all this is leading and, to be sure, sometimes I just rattle on and on. I'm just me. Not perfect, nor do I even want to be. I don't mind being admired and I definitely want to be loved, but I truly attempt to just be who I am. I love people, but I also do dumb things and sometimes I beat myself up emotionally over my mistakes and sometimes I cut me some slack.

I'm not going to prostitute truth or my spiritual experiences for a selfish gain. I'm here, living my life for the world, to share in any way I can. I'm not here to receive; I give without measure. In whatever form it returns to me is okay. Maybe I'm building up treasures in heaven (consciousness).

Human nature wants to take; spiritual nature wants to give. Money or gifts may appear to come from man, but in truth—God gives man the impulse to give.

I recently wrote lyrics for a song for my husband. One of the lines in it is, "I give because I receive, I give so I have more. My heartfelt love runneth over, for you, my heart sings and soars!"

All that comes to you, must come from within. Let it flow and never seek to have it come to you. Surrender and heal your human judgments. Make yourself a life of giving, not one of getting, accomplishing, or achieving.

This example may seem a little trite or overused, but for me, it explains everything so very clearly: $2 + 2 = 4$. It's an already established fact, isn't it? You don't have to prove it. In your knowingness, $2 + 2$ *is* 4. In your mind, you have no doubts, no confusion, and no one has to convince you of it. You already know it to be true.

If you add $2 + 2$ and your answer is 5, it would be an error, not a sin. If you've lived with lack, disease, anger, hatred, or other dys-functions, they are not sins either. They are errors in human per-ception. The Light erases the error and restores your life to right action. Not something you have to humanly attempt to do, but al-lowing the gifts that already exist within you to flow into your vi-sual outer world of form.

I already know the spiritual world, where all is perfect and true. Your perfection, on all levels—physically, financially, emotionally, mentally, morally and spiritually—already exists. I have seen the whole picture, and everything that a human would ever want al-ready exists. It's an already established spiritual fact, just like the fact that $2 + 2 = 4$.

It's all adding up, one can easily see, perfection already exists in spiritual reality. (I'm a poet.) If I say this again, it's not to be a bro-ken record—it's so that you begin accepting the truth.

There is only one power, one presence, one experience, unless you are mesmerized by the world suggestion that there are dual powers. You can argue that there are two powers and that's why you see insanity (in various disguises) surrounding you and the world at large. These appearances are man's awareness made man-ifest.

I can't argue with you. As a spiritual healer, I've heard and seen some grotesque, painful situations for people. I have witnessed dis-eases and read painful requests. I have cried and hurt so badly that I wondered how those I worked on could stand their discomforts for years, and wondered if it had been mine to carry, would I have long ago chosen suicide as a release?

I'm not asking you to bury your heads and ignore the world. I'm asking you, for a moment, to consider that our ancestors (through unawareness/ignorance) lied to us. Okay, maybe "lied" is a strong word. (Perhaps they just didn't tell us the truth, the whole truth, and nothing but the truth!) We're told that the government hides information from us that we're not ready to know about. That's easier to believe than being told that our government is looking out for our best interests.

Politically speaking, it's your choice to stand behind your gov-ernment and support the foundation on which it is built, above and beyond the individual egos that attempt to lead us. A world leader once said that he didn't need to destroy the United States because, in time, we would destroy ourselves. (Not if you or I have a say in the matter!)

Religiously speaking, we are given the Bible and are given interpretations, via others, as to how we should live and what we are to believe. I'm not asking you to forsake your religious beliefs or stop going to church. I'm asking you to spiritually discern and allow God to guide you. I am a messenger, a guide in the physical, and like all others, I am a personality cloaked in human form. I don't want you to follow me because I'm not always sure where I'm headed. However, I don't want you to follow others either. Look within and allow your inner voice to lead you.

A woman shared this story with me recently. A mother was telling her small child to not be afraid of the dark because God was with him. The child replied, "But, I just want someone with skin on." As an adult child, I look to all others and see aspects of God. I, too, need someone with skin on.

I love you and I'll be honest with you. I have good days and bad days, because I'm still healing judgments, also. Even those judgments that appear good. But, I've watched my life be transformed by practicing this technique over the years and I know that each day of dissolving human judgments makes my present and future even brighter and more exciting.

Don't be overwhelmed that your life can't change or fear that it's too late to enjoy the fruit of spirit. In the twinkling of an eye, your life can be healed, your soul restored, and your mind healed of error (not sin!). Remember, 2 + 2 is always going to be 4. In God's eyes, you are always going to be His child (and He doesn't make mistakes).

I'm rambling again, aren't I? I need to get the table set for dinner, Kirk will be home any minute now. Please tell me, you will stay for dinner, won't you?

CHAPTER 16

Conquering fear . . .

Excuse me for a moment, please. I need to let Danielle's friend, Chelsea, know that her parents are here to pick her up. I babysat for Chelsea for years, and she's like a sister to Danielle. While Chelsea is getting her things together, I'd love to introduce her parents to you. Jim and Joan are, by appearances, just ordinary people. However, they are two people who deeply affect the lives of others, from their children to total strangers.

Joan, by hobby (and heart), is a writer. We met many years ago through our daughters and allowed the friendship to grow. One Halloween, as we walked our kids around the neighborhood, Joan began sharing that her manuscript was also written about a spiritual healer, though she hadn't read any metaphysical or spiritual books to inspire the story.

She asked if I would be willing to read her book, *Beneath the Moon of Blue* and confirm that the main character was offering valid information. I read her story, with delight, in tremendous awe because with no researching, Joan had written the truth. I look forward to the day that Joan's book is printed and reaches out to touch others.

Jim, like Kirk, is one of the best and most devoted fathers I've ever met. Their family is secure in love and one another. Kirk and

I don't have a great quantity of close friends, but the quality of people we include in our lives is exceptional.

In our small town, we have one grocery store and, once a year, the owner has a customer appreciation night. He sets out bales of hay in the parking lot, hires a band, and, free to the public, he and his employees serve massive amounts of free food, drink, and entertainment. No alcohol is allowed, but somehow that doesn't matter. Four years ago, when I moved to Montana, Kirk took the family to this night out and I was and have continued to be impressed that a small-town grocery store would do such a gracious act for the community.

One summer, at this event, our family walked over to the grocery store and I noticed Jim, Joan, and their kids in the line. Even from a distance, I could see that something was terribly wrong with Jim. I made my way through the crowd and came face-to-face with him, asking if everything was okay.

He was in shock. Since I feel exactly what other people feel, I knew there were tears behind whatever had just occurred because a lump appeared in my throat. Even before I heard what had happened, I felt like I needed to cry. He began to share his story, briefly, about how he had witnessed a young man being hit by a car on his way home from work.

I could feel such pain. I offered him a hug, and then Kirk and I offered to take his daughter, Chelsea, for the evening so he could have some quiet time to process what he had seen. Jim had saved this boy's life, with CPR.

In the following days, I could see that Jim still wasn't able to handle the situation. He works in the print shop at the hospital where this boy had been taken. I'm sure he made many silent trips to check on the young man. Jim was reliving the experience over and over (day and night), and was walking on eggshells. He was anxiously waiting to hear not only that would the boy live, but that he wouldn't have brain damage or any long-term effects.

Each time I thought of the experience, I must have been tapping into Jim's feelings. I believed that a modern-day fairy tale needed to be written for a modern-day hero. In my eyes, Jim had become:

The Champion

(Dedicated to James Graham Rhodda)

Once upon a present-day time, a gentleman named Sir James found his mind filled with events and experiences that had occurred in his life. He pondered the meaning of opportunities, incidents, and life. It had only been recently that he had been shown, through a twist of fate, that a person is always where he needs to be at any given moment in life.

A CPR class was being offered in his workplace. Sir James's career path did not warrant such training, however, a strong and overwhelming feeling from within urged him to attend. Aware that knowledge is power, he attended the sessions that would soon reveal that we always have everything we need, usually before we are aware we need it.

The day of the drama and trauma began as every other day. James awoke with his beautiful lady, Joan Elizabeth, in his arms. He had awakened from dreamtime, only to look into the very eyes of his dream come true.

They awakened their children, Brad and Chelsea, encouraging them to have a beautiful day. Promising to return early that eve to spend quality time together as a family, James and Joan Elizabeth kissed good-bye and journeyed respectively to the marketplace.

From that moment forward, unseen events changed the course of time. Her position required staying later than normal and Sir James found himself alone on the road, traveling toward home, hours earlier than his expected arrival time.

The afternoon was scorchingly hot and on the ride home James removed his shoes. Feeling cooler, he stretched his toes and continued along the country road. The beautiful valley in which he lived mesmerized him. He continued to travel the road that trailed beside a river that was nestled behind the trees.

In the distance, far ahead of him, he witnessed three young boys riding bicycles. From afar, he beheld their youthful bodies, bared and bronzed. The royal coach before him slowed and moved to the far-left lane to pass the youngsters. As if time froze, he watched as the drama unfolded.

Two of the boys, hearing oncoming traffic rode toward the shoulder of the road. The third lad, unaware of the approaching vehicle, chose at that instant to cross to the opposite side of the road.

Sir James braked and stopped immediately, watching as the vehicle before him collided with the lad. He watched the nightmare, almost as if it was happening in slow motion. His heart seemed to stop. It was as if he'd forgotten to breathe. He witnessed the boy plummeting through the air as if he was a rag doll.

Helpless, James watched as the young man, near his own son's age, landed lifelessly on the pavement before him. Adrenaline filled him as he ran to the child. The pavement beneath his feet was blistering hot and yet, he knew that if he had to walk on hot coals to save this child's life, he would willingly do so.

Sir James checked for a pulse and there was none. Knowing that if there were chest injuries and he began the compression of CPR, he could crush the boy's lungs. Trusting that, at present, there was no choice, he joined his lips to the youngster's and prayed for him to breathe again.

As taught, he breathed the breath of life and compressed the chest in even counts. All bystanders, in deep shock, felt gratitude that a passing stranger could take physical steps to do something, for their own private fears had paralyzed them from performing what they were unprepared to do.

Moments that felt like eternity passed and the boy sputtered, coughed, and gasped for air. James's heart felt secure enough to leave the boy and he ran like the wind to the nearest house to get emergency personnel to the scene.

As James returned to the accident scene, his mind was racing with countless thoughts. He was in deep gratitude that he had learned the technique to save a life, and he was also in awe that he had been at the right place at the right moment, for the boy would have died without his intervention.

What on earth was this young man destined to perform? Mighty works or inventions? Perhaps he would one day grow to be a president or a great leader. Whatever had turned back the hands of time for Sir James to be present, in this moment, may forever remain a mystery. What he was aware of, was that fate or destiny, or whatever you might call it, had indeed, intervened and changed the actual course of history.

As James reached the scene of the accident, he was informed that only moments ago, the young child had stopped breathing again. He looked at the boy, lying lifeless on the pavement and adrenaline, that pure power of God, flowed as once before throughout his veins. As he knelt to the lips of the boy a second time, he viewed the broken skull, and tears came to his eyes as he prayed, "Use me, dear Lord, as Your instrument. Through me, breathe life into this child!"

As once before, with steady rhythms of compressions and breathing, the lad coughed and breathed. However, with the circulation of blood, his open wound spurted his life force upon the ground. Onlookers screamed at the sight and dear Sir James pleaded, "Please! Please don't scream! Please don't scream! This is good, the boy will live!"

The call for aid brought Life Flight and with mighty wings, the boy was taken higher and higher, almost as if kissed by the angels. The boy would live and he would grow to be a man, without meeting the stranger who had been used by the divine to grace him with life.

Deep in shock from the day's events, James couldn't erase the memories. Days and then weeks passed and the memories haunted him, until one quiet evening when Joan Elizabeth asked him to join her for a walk under the moon and stars.

As they walked hand in hand through the clover, she quietly spoke, "Do you remember when we were courting and came upon a mud puddle in the road and I teasingly asked if you were going to gallantly place your cloak upon it so I wouldn't soil my shoes?" Sir James smiled as he recalled the memory.

She continued, "You didn't lay your cape on the ground. Instead, you swept me off my feet and while being held in your arms, I knew then that your strength would lift us above any obstacle in life. I believed in you and have always known that you're much more powerful than even you are aware. When you shared your experience of that day, I also knew that the divine only gives a soul as much as he can withstand. Sometimes He has to push us beyond our comfortable limits in attempts to force us to grow."

She went on, "This experience taught you to see beyond the physical. In that moment, you looked only to that which is invisible for your source, supply, and strength. This child gave you a priceless spiritual gift, the gift of realizing that God is ever-present and all-powerful. You, Sir James, have felt the presence of God that countless souls seek. The worldly was transcended and a miracle occurred. You're much more than just a gallant man, you're a hero . . . perhaps unsung, but I've got a pretty good idea how He'll continue to use you in His choir of angels."

The only ending is in continuing to allow acts of great courage to go unnoticed and without mention. The true beginning is accepting that no medal of honor was placed upon Sir James's chest, but that the man and his deed shall go down in history merely from the purity in conduct and intention. To the ladies and gentlemen of the world, to each person of superior standing who seeks to do good, not for the expected reward, fame, or credit, but because he or she is willing to get involved, in good name, in good faith, and with public esteem, you are thanked.

To those who seek aggrandizement or glory for deeds, to those who stand before others professing their good deeds, they have received their just reward. To those who selflessly give service and aid and walk humbly away without reward or compensation, blessed are they before the Heaven's watchful eye. They, my friends, are the true champions of the world, the ultimate winners in the game of life.

Every time I tell that story, I get weepy. I know how Jim felt, I've felt it myself when someone comes to me with a life-threatening condition or disease. I'd be lying if I didn't admit that I've had human fear in certain situations, but again, I'm not effective if I'm afraid. I've even been told by people, "Thank you for saving my life. I would have died if it wasn't for you."

I humbly share that it was God who saved the life and then the person responds, "Yes, it was God who saved my life, but it was you who plugged into Him so He could." It's just so much easier giving God credit for the gifts, energy, love, or giving credit to my friend, Nikki, for her artwork, believing that her drawings make my words prettier. What we must always understand is that God *is* to receive the glory, but we, as individual expressions of Him, as His instruments, are just as necessary.

I once had a woman sitting in my home, receiving inspiration directly while I was preparing my evening meal. As I finished speaking, her voice was almost a whisper of awe and she said, "My goodness, Gloria, you've got God in one hand and meatloaf in the other." It's the natural way, so simple if you allow it to be.

The only thing that keeps us separate from God on a moment-to-moment basis are the false fear-based teachings that we're not good enough or haven't earned the right. Each fear that you feel is a golden opportunity to surrender the judgment that it has power for good or bad. God is love. Fear or pain is the absence of it in your life. Each fear can be replaced with love and each fear healed empowers you to carry more Light, to be more confident, to live healthier and happier.

Fear can be conquered without resistance. If we deny fear or attempt to defend it, we will continue to attract those situations. Surrender! Completely surrender from attempting to do things by taking thought, by "being human," and having to do and learn everything the hard way. I promise you won't be let down once you truly give up.

CHAPTER 17

The Reluctant Messiah

I have enough time, before dinner, to make another rum cake. Around the holidays, I like to share this favorite dessert with friends and loved ones. I've been known to make twenty-one of them at a time. (I told you I like to cook and bake, didn't I? I wasn't kidding. I suppose if I wasn't going to be a spiritual healer and author, I'd probably go into the catering business or open a restaurant. I'd be in seventh heaven owning a restaurant and preparing food for masses of people.)

It's easier, it seems, for people to be saturated in negative events than in positive ones. Both can be overwhelming, I'm sure. Like Kirk said, I overwhelm people at times, and that occurs with positive experiences.

For example, many years ago, around the holidays, I sent out Christmas cards to loved ones and I enclosed a letter stating one thing that had happened for each member of our family: Kirk, the kids, Nikki (my "con" artist), and myself.

Following the holidays, my sister, Terry, called me from Colorado and said, "I talked about you behind your back on Christmas day, so I thought I'd better share it firsthand with you before someone else in the family does." Her words pierced my little heart and then broke it in half. (Is that a little dramatic or what?) She said, "If you would have said one more positive thing about your life in that Christmas card insert, I would have puked!" (Pretty basic and down-to-earth, wouldn't you admit? Terry never had a hard time sharing any of her thoughts or feelings while growing up.)

I had only touched the tip of the iceberg in sharing with friends and family. What would it have been like if I'd really gone into detail? To you, my friend, on this holiday, I'll share what I sent out the next year with my Christmas cards and you tell me if it's still too much to handle.

We're going to be brief, "Oh, what's that you say?"
Just sharing our glad tiding to help brighten your day.
It's difficult to be clever in just a few lines,
Weaving our experiences in riddles and rhymes.

Kirk's hair and beard has whitened over the years,
I guess that's what happens when life shifts to high gear.
Our lives have accelerated and we're going full speed,
Sometimes he just hangs on tight and follows my lead.

And, just when the rat race starts to subside,
Kirk and I agree to take another ride.
A road trip, a plane trip, across the States, or Hawaii,
The action is nonstop, on that we'll all agree!

Kerrie's in love with a man from Purdue,
A junior, like her, who has dreams and visions, too.
She's bringing him home on spring break to meet Mom and Dad.
To hear her speak of him, he's totally (and I mean totally) rad!

Jaime got "senioritis" but is cured of it, I'm sure,
She moved out of our home in a lightning-paced blur.
She got her own place, experiencing reality firsthand,
Spreading her little wings and taking an adult stand.

D.W., overnight, became a strong, handsome young man,
Who weightlifts his sister every chance he can!
Are we ready for this? Next month he turns thirteen!
Just yesterday I held him in my lap (or anyway, so it seems).

Danielle's still a gymnast, part monkey we'd agree.
Swinging from the bars and climbing our front yard tree.
She's a beautiful young lady, kind and loving, too.
Ten going on twenty—what are parents to do?

Me? I've been ordained as a minister and written two more books.
I continue to travel to teach, heal, clean, do laundry, and cook.
To do all I want to do, there aren't enough hours in a day,
So, I just live every moment to the fullest in each possible way.

Next month, I'm flying the friendly skies to retrieve my friend,
Nikki, my (con) artist whose prison sentence comes to an end.
We received approval for interstate parole, you see.
Our long-held, six-year dream now becomes reality!

To you and yours, we wish you special holiday greetings and good
cheer,
Throughout this and every single day of your new year.
May God bless you and watch over you now and always,
May His Light and loving presence fill all your future days!

So, does it make you wanna throw up or did I do good that year?
I love this time of year! I think Christmas is the best holiday of
all. Other holidays are linked with love, but none as special as
December 25. When they were younger, around this same time,
D.W. and Danielle were arguing at breakfast, each one attempting
to make the other's life a living hell. (I still have judgments against
fighting or being mean for the sake of being mean, but I'm working
on it.)

At the breakfast table, however, these two children were fighting and when the words turned hateful, the argument went above

and beyond that point that I could overlook it. When I heard the threat, "I'll just shake all your gifts under the tree until they break," I lost it! I loaded them into the car (trapping them, you see) to head to school and, along the way, I scolded them.

I explained that Christmas is the time of year, more than ever, to be kind, caring, sharing, and loving, and if they weren't aware of this message or the reason behind it, then perhaps I should give their gifts to someone who would appreciate them.

I'm sure that some psychologist wouldn't have agreed with the way I handled the situation, but that's tough. Allowing anyone to be outright hateful is not acceptable, nor is it loving to do so. (Remember, kids need discipline and consistency, and they need to know what their boundaries are.)

After I dropped the kids at the school, I returned home to do my holiday baking. I felt so much disappointment, regret, and bitterness over the fight, and I knew that I couldn't continue to have those feelings and attempt to make cookies and banana-nut breads. My bitterness would flow into the baking and it wouldn't be fit to eat. (I'm speaking from experience. Long ago, I was making a roast while I was processing anger and when it came time to eat it, not only could the meat not be cut, but it was literally bitter to the taste. I learned quickly never to do that again.)

I stopped mixing and baking and sat at the table with pen in hand. I made a silent request for God to allow love to flow through me in the form of words. I was asking for something to inspire, not only myself, but the world as well.

The following was what flowed from me in approximately twenty minutes:

The Reluctant Messiah

Once upon a time, a small child named Charity was born into a middle-class family. She had two elder siblings she admired and loved. As the years passed, two more children were born into the family. Each member had individual personalities, and they each would be asked to be and do something for the world.

As the years passed, however, and Charity grew she was the smallest of her age group. Being so tiny, her parents and family overprotected and guarded her so that no harm should ever touch her life.

Early in her teens, Charity became confused about life. It appeared that each person reached a certain age, attained a career and worked hard, but placed more attention upon Golden Years where they could relax and enjoy life. She watched as most struggled to get shelter, food, and clothing, and yet this struggle was contradictory to what she felt in her heart. She wanted to find and share the secret to enjoying every moment of life.

It also appeared that the stress of providing the physical needs consumed time and energy, denying a moment to devote to the spiritual life. At the end of a long and tiring day, each was left exhausted, with no energy for self-realization.

Even as a child, Charity was a lover, not a fighter. When she heard her parents, immediate family members, or friends argue, she would immediately adopt the role as peacemaker. As a sensitive child, the energy of anger was ragged and she could literally feel the sword of tongues cutting others to the bone. Charity could never understand people being mean for the sake of just being mean.

With wrinkled brow and hours of searching for an answer, Charity continued to know only confusion about one of life's greatest mysteries. How was it that on the holiday of Thanksgiving, that day when each heart should be filled with gratitude, that the only thing most people felt was thankfulness that it was over? So much effort gone into preparing a meal, a meal where people were given a day to overindulge, that rather than feeling thankfulness for the abundance and plenty of God's grace, that the essence of the day was lost.

Charity listened to the masses of people who believed in the celebration of the birth of Christ and felt dismayed for the reason behind the giving. Parents threatened children that Santa wouldn't come if they were naughty and siblings fought and bickered constantly during the twelve days of Christmas.

Charity believed that any gift given, without love, was worthless, no matter the price.

Charity was aware that the holidays sometimes led to depression, suicide, stress, overextended credit, anger, and fear. For what purpose, besides commercialism, did the holidays exist? Rather than bringing good will toward man, holidays brought debt and exhaustion. Rather than peace and love, these special days brought warring among families and fear among strangers. Had Christmas just become another holiday that people were thankful was over?

Daily, on her way home from the hustle and bustle of the marketplace, Charity passed a church whose bells rang daily at noon and in the early evening. Decorated for the Christmas Mass that would soon be coming, she admired a manger scene surrounded by the new-fallen snow. Lovely lights accentuated the cradle in which the Christ Child lay. Bright and brilliantly colored wooden forms of the Three Wise Men, Joseph, and Mary stood surrounding the child. The artist had made the lambs and cattle look alive. In fact, the entire scene seemed so very, very real.

Each day, when she passed, for some unknown reason, the manger scene looked even more beautiful and real. Charity looked forward to this part of her day, when her heart, worries, concerns, and fears were healed. Each eve, happy tears would come to her eyes, for she could feel so much love emanating from the still forms of images of a so long ago time.

Not being an especially religious person, insofar as ever stepping over the threshold of a church, she knew the story of Christ, but never ventured into various beliefs or discussions with others concerning it. Too many interpretations and lost messages . . . Charity didn't feel the need to enter a physical building to worship, for she carried her church and love for God in her heart and took it everywhere she went.

On the eve of Christmas, Charity walked past the church, listening to the snow crunch beneath her feet. In the brisk cold, she could see her breath and she snuggled her hands together deeper into the white fur muff that matched her hat.

As the church bells rang, she could hear the practicing choir that would be singing at Mass later that evening. The tones were vibrant and heavenly. She slowed her pace so she could continue to hear the choir of angels.

Charity's attention was drawn to the sky as she watched a brilliant blue-white star appear. It, at first, appeared to be a beacon, boldly getting brighter and brighter and then dimmer. Casting its light, downward toward earth, it spotlighted the manger scene. Charity, in awe of the beautiful moment and event, returned to stand before the manger.

The Virgin Mary, Joseph, the Christ Child, and the Three Wise Men, for one holy moment, appeared to come to life. Rubbing her eyes, she looked again and it must have been her imagination, for the painted wooden figures, outlined in light, stood coldly without life.

Returning home, Charity attempted to tell her family of the experience, but none had the time to listen. Busily preparing the fish feast, wrapping gifts, and putting on finishing touches before guests arrived took precedence.

All through the night's ceremony of tradition, Charity remained silent, still in awe of what she'd witnessed in that bright and shining star. Deep in her heart, she knew those wooden figures had come to life, though she knew not what it meant. To share these details of her experience would only lead to ridicule and adversity. Therefore, she chose to remain silent.

At the close of the evening, Charity hugged the last, departing guest, but before she closed the door, she took one final look at the midnight sky. Countless stars sparkled, but none like the one she had seen earlier.

As Charity snuggled under her pink satin comforter, she once again recalled the star and the experience she had in her mind. It was something she would remember for as long as she lived. And with those thoughts, she slumbered.

Hours before the cock crowed, Charity was awakened with the sense of purity filling her nostrils and mouth. From where it came, she knew not, but somehow, from deep within herself, the sensation arose.

She opened her eyes abruptly for a shining light appeared, almost as if a match had been struck in the darkest hour. Standing before Charity was an angel of shimmering light, outlined with a blue aura. The angel's wings were extended in full position, reaching from one wall to the other, casting a sparkling glow about the room. Twinkles of gold danced in the air each time a single feather moved.

In a soft melodic voice, the angel spoke: "It only takes one holy moment for the Christ to become real and a soul's life is instantly changed. Take no thought for what you shall wear, what you shall eat, or what you will speak, be at peace. You, child, are a Messiah—go forth and demonstrate the love in your heart, for divine love will liberate all peoples and all nations. Listen to the message you share and you will hear Him speak. Go forth, child, fear not, for lo, I am with you always."

The angel disappeared before Charity could ask questions, and she, to some extent, disbelieved what had just occurred. She lay awake, all through the rest of the night, memorizing the angel's words. By first light, Charity had convinced herself that the experience was but a dream. Yes, it was only a dream.

Charity pushed back her comforter, placed her feet on the floor, and reached down to get her slippers. Inside was a golden-lettered message, "Just in case you talked yourself into believing our meeting was a dream, here is a physical reminder to have and to hold." Attached to the note was a single, beautiful white angel feather.

Throughout that day, Charity analyzed the experience and message of Christmas Eve. With her limited knowledge, she didn't even know what "Messiah" meant, except to be a miracle worker for God, and no one, not even God, Himself, had asked if she wanted the job. Another seeker may have felt blessed, but in ignorance, Charity didn't.

She hadn't looked into the "Help Wanted" section, nor had she interviewed for such a position in life. She silently questioned the invisible, "Do you have any idea what happens to messengers you send into this world? Thank you very much, but I think I'll pass." After all, she did know about free will.

That evening, when she retired, another feather lay quietly on her pillow . . .

As the days passed and turned into weeks, Charity realized that undesirable human qualities and traits of her personality began falling away . . . with no effort of her own. A peace that passeth all human understanding filled her heart, mind, and soul.

Modern-day miracles began occurring, sometimes with the slightest touch and sometimes with no touch at all. Miracles, delivered through a genuine smile to a passerby, occurred as she tasted and smelled the purity in her senses.

The invisible word, "Messiah" hung over her head and silently shouted itself into her mind. She had dreams of standing before thousands of people, each of whom went away healed.

But to boldly state the word of God to others would bring adversity and opposition from those who could not yet understand. So, Charity lived a silent life, with the promise of He who performed the greater works through her. She lived with the greatest secret of all.

Nine years of miracle working had passed, and once again, she returned to the church that had the manger scene. Christmas was just around the corner.

The silver bells, high in the steeple, began ringing with rich full tones of beauty. Kneeling before the manger, Charity bowed her head in deep reverence to the baby that once grew to a man, and who, like her, had been asked to share the message of Christ's Light and love with the world, a man, who had individualized the presence of God and allowed that presence to transcend human kindness, caring, sharing, and loving.

Filled with love, which her human form could barely hold, a prayer to humankind sprang forth from her mind, which had become an avenue of awareness for the divine.

"May the blessed peace of God fill your mind and flood your soul with His all-powerful, all-loving presence. No laws of disease, nor matter, no laws of weather or beliefs of imperfection can operate in the mind, which has become the instrument of God. If I can give the world the greatest gift of all for this holiday season, it's one that money can't buy. I give you the gift of awareness that through a peaceful state of mind, the grace of God appears and by His grace, He lives and breathes through you."

Charity, in that moment realized why she had been reluctant in her service to God and man. She feared that if others knew her secret, they would line up for blocks to be in her presence, to receive miracles. She then realized that, as "Messiah," she was merely to demonstrate it as one of so long ago, and to teach that all can do as He who sent her. Christ had been not only the messenger, but the message, as well. Charity had sacrificed nothing worldly to be His servant and tool, to unconsciously give and share daily.

Giving could not deplete her, nor the world, for love is infinite. To be used for His purposes, she had given her mind, body, and soul to God. Her individual mind, that which could not be taken away or stolen, the only true thing she possessed, she willingly gave to He who created her.

The ending? Only to stress, anger, exhaustion, and believing there isn't enough money, time, and energy. The beginning? Peace, the peace that passeth all human understanding. It begins with one and then another and another, until each is healed of fears and can freely give of themselves in loving ways no matter the day. Peace and offering it to others begins within our hearts and minds. Like true Charity, it begins at home.

That, tale, my friend, happens to be one of my favorites and will be also included in my book, *Dream Catchers*, which will follow this one. I would love to be able to share how each fairy tale has been inspired. I've written hundreds of personalized fairy tales over the last ten years.

Can you imagine? "The Reluctant Messiah" was inspired because my kids were fighting? Good or bad, who's to say? Sometimes, we just don't see the whole picture.

While the rum cake is baking, I'm going to listen to the answering machine so I can return calls. While I'm doing that, why don't you join the kids down in the TV room? Their movie is over and you can challenge them to a computer game. While you're down there, ask D.W. and Danielle to choose which one wants to set the table and which will clear it afterward.

Hope you're hungry, dinner is in about thirty minutes.

CHAPTER 18

. . . *Throughout Eternity*

Dinner is served! Why don't you sit next to Kirk tonight? I know this is a tiny table, was meant for only four, but we've squeezed as many as nine in at this table. My kids have always liked having their friends for dinner, and I liked having them, too.

One afternoon, Jaime brought a friend home whom I'd never met before. When they walked in after school, I was just taking homemade dinner rolls out of the oven, so I'm sure it smelled heavenly in here. I had made and frosted brownies earlier that day for an after-school snack and offered some to Jaime and her friend.

The teen, with an amazed look on her face, said, "Gosh, you're just like a *real* mom!" Jaime laughed and picked me up off the floor, swinging me around several times, responding, "She *is* a real mom, and who would have ever thought I'd be playing with her like this?"

Kirk can start dipping out the steak stew and I'll slice this warm homemade bread. Maybe Danielle could get a new pack of butter out of the fridge for us? Dinner is simpler around here than it used to be. I had such a need to cook and have people eat, that I went overboard when I first married Kirk. He laughs and teases me that he gained an extra thirty pounds after he married me.

I gained about twenty pounds after marrying him and being

nurtured by my knight in shining armor. I know he doesn't want me to write about our sex life, but being me, I have to tell you this or I'll explode. When I first moved to Montana, I was recovering from anorexia and I was totally flat-chested. In fact, my bony butt would leave bruises on him if I sat on his lap. I started becoming very well endowed from Kirk's caresses and, when I realized what was happening, I insisted that he keep his hands *off* my hiney!

Kirk teases me because he doesn't think I can keep a secret. Spirit, in meditation, one afternoon asked me, "Can you keep a secret?" I thought about it and had to be honest because of you know who. I truthfully sent a silent thought His way, You know me better than anyone. If what you or another tells me, can help anyone else, you can be assured I'll stand high atop a mountain shouting it to others! (Perhaps I didn't pass a test and maybe . . . just maybe, I did!) I don't feel like there are any secrets in this universe anyway.

Please save room for dessert. I have a weakness for Turtle sundaes and now that I think about it, we'll have them a little later, just before the kids go to bed.

While Danielle is clearing the table, I'd like to take you for another walk around the neighborhood now that it's dark. Roco, our sheltie, will feel special getting a second walk! No kids tonight, just you and me. I'm sure you'll enjoy seeing all the different decorations that our neighbors and we have out during this holiday.

With all the lights on our home and in the yard, it looks a little bit like overkill, doesn't it? I remember how our son D.W., always loved to be creative, and we were so proud of his time and effort to make the Benish home look pretty for all those who drove by.

Even today, the candy canes that line our yard and driveway are cheery and heartwarming. Kirk made them from scratch. He used plastic white pipe, filled them with sand, and then heated the plastic with boiling water to bend into the candy cane shape. He then used red PVC tape to stripe them. Surprisingly enough, he spent an entire day creating all these candy canes, and the next time we were in the stores for the holiday shopping, we saw them for sale! (Imagine that!)

In the early years of my ministry, I started going out on promotion tours in October. While I was out for the weekends, Kirk spent those days with the kids drawing and cutting figures out of wood. D.W. and Danielle helped paint them the bright colors, and they're both so proud of their work.

The spotlight on the roof is still on Santa, stuck in the fireplace. Kirk animated two of the elves, swinging their hammers in an attempt to chip away the bricks. Look how Rudolph's nose flashes and what a smirk he has on his face, seeing Santa in such a predicament.

I happen to like the children caroling under our living room window. There was so much love put into creating them that when I see them (and their dog howling at the moon) it makes me want to break into Christmas song. (Okay, so you don't deserve that, especially at this time of year! I thought about recording some songs and selling them to bars or auditoriums to play at quitting time and clear people out.)

I think D.W.'s favorite wooden cutout was the life-sized tree that he decorated with real lights, ornaments, and garlands. The two little children figures decorating the tree were dressed in footie pajamas (and it was D.W.'s idea for the second child, who's bending over, to have his trap door opened so you can see his crackers.)

Tonight, it is such a beautiful night, the moon is shining brightly on the snow-capped peak of St. Mary's. I love the snow and crispness in the air.

I also love to hear the snow crunch beneath our feet. You don't have snow boots on, so be careful where you step so you don't slip on any ice and fall on your keester. Are you warm enough for this walk? We won't stay out for long, we'll just walk the three streets surrounding our neighborhood.

You know, I already told you I can't keep a secret, but I've done a pretty good job for almost three months now. In just a few days, I won't have to be silent any longer. Would you mind very much if I share it with you?

One day, Kirk was telling me that, in his opinion, I would be great at writing lyrics for a song. He told me that he believed I could write beautiful poetry, continuing to explain that that's all the lyrics to songs are. He asked me to write a song and I said, "Okay, I will."

Months went by and I didn't make an attempt. It wasn't like it was a big priority in my life. He brought the idea up again. When he suggested it the second time, he said, "In fact, I would like you to write *me* a song."

He knew that would do it. I'd do anything for him. He said, "In fact, I think you should write the music that goes with it." Since I had seven years of piano lessons as a child, I figured that I could probably do that, also. I agreed to do it.

In a sarcastic tone (because I sing so badly) he completed his request with, "And, I'd like you to sing it for me, too." I surprised him by saying, "Okay, I will." Immediately, he countered my gracious offer with, "No, really, you don't have to do that," but I insisted that I would. Kirk, about that time, got very quiet—so silent, I thought something was seriously wrong. Following his pause, he said, "Gloria, I feel so bad for asking you to do this. You already give so much, I can't believe I asked for more." I laughed, "Ha. And there's the title for it."

Still, the months passed and I didn't do anything about it. One afternoon, in meditation, it dawned on me why Kirk would have requested me to write a song for him. I sent a silent thought to God, "God, I know that Kirk would have never asked me to do this unless the song was already written. Use me and write the words through me, so I can have them to give him in the physical form." Ten minutes later, the words to the song were physical.

I sat at the organ for an afternoon and played whatever wanted to be played through my fingers. Some of the melodies were beautiful, but I couldn't play them and write them on sheet music at the same time. I momentarily thought that I had bitten off more than I could chew. Yet, I know me. I'm a woman of my word, and I will do whatever I commit to do. After all, though I hadn't said, "I promise and cross my heart," I had committed and said I would do it. I would find a way.

I went within and meditated. Well, maybe "meditated" isn't the right word because I'm not sure if I even know how to meditate. (Quit laughing!) In my quiet time, I just said, "Okay, God, I know that you're the author of life and that poem, I also know that there's no separation and You are the one who will write the music. I open my mind to be used, as the means through which you will manifest outwardly as a person to do the next step of writing the music to go with these words." That's it. It's that simple. I saw the violet Light and knew that it would be taken care of. Without human effort or trying to figure it out.

Days later, I was in the beauty shop getting my hair cut and I was sharing with the owner, Sharon, what I was up to. She looked at me, almost like she was in shock, and said, "Gloria, Rhonda [my hairdresser] is a singer! She could sing it for you." Rhonda and I just looked at each other as goosebumps rolled through us.

I asked if she would be willing to read the poem and see if she would be interested, sharing that there was no way that I would ever sing it for Kirk. He knew and I knew that would *never* become a reality. Rhonda agreed, excitedly in fact, telling me also that she had a friend, named Cathy, who harmonized with her. When my hair was finished being styled, I told Rhonda that I would run home and get the poem for her and would return in five minutes.

When I returned, I was introduced to Cathy, who just happened to drop into the shop, unannounced and without a reason. They read the poem and offered to take it home and play around with the guitar and see what they could come up with.

I left for Spokane on a workshop trip and, when I returned home, they had renamed my song, "I Can't Believe I Asked for More," to "Throughout Eternity." Cathy and Rhonda had also written the music and, sitting on the floor in the back room of the beauty shop, I leaned back against the dryer and listened to these two women sing Kirk's song to me for the first time.

The three of us joined hands, as partners, to get this song on a tape to be placed in Kirk's Christmas stocking. A music arranger played the instrumental background and blended it with their guitar and in a professional studio. A dream became reality.

Let's head back to the house and I'll let you sit in my car and I'll play it for you.

Throughout Eternity

You asked me to write and sing a song for you,
Don't you realize, Honey, that's so easy to do?
You asked me to give you a chance, proposing your life,
You made my every dream come true when I became your wife.

(Chorus)
Words of yours fill my mind, as I walk the forest floor,
"You've given so much already, I can't believe I asked for more."
If the world wants a fairy tale, why not start with you and me?
I'll give to you my heart and soul, throughout eternity.

I think of you, my love, as I walk the forest floor,
My love runs over for you, as my heart sings and soars.
While the sun shines through the trees, your presence surrounds me,
I'll hear the songs of nature, the wildlife, birds and bees.

(Chorus)
Words of yours fill my mind, as I walk the forest floor,
"You've given so much already, I can't believe I asked for more."
If the world wants a fairy tale, why not start with you and me?
I'll give to you my heart and soul, throughout eternity.

I gaze into the skies and feel a breeze upon my cheek,
I glance below the waterfall, to watch the winding creek.
Liquid light cascades to the canyon down below,
Misting the autumn forest with a golden glow.

(Chorus)
Words of yours fill my mind as I walk the forest floor,
"You've given so much already, I can't believe I asked for more."
If the world wants a fairy tale, why not start with you and me?
I'll give to you my heart and soul, throughout eternity.

You asked me to write and sing this song for you,
Now I hope you realize, I'd do anything for you.

I really love that man! He's just so incredible, he can do any-thing. Before Kirk married me, he was the Mom, Dad, the "bring home the bacon, fry it up in a pan" man of the house, caring for his two daughters alone. He had just started his own business, Bitterroot Carriage Company, where he and his brother, Bill, cre-ated horse-drawn sleighs and carriages. Kirk has made his unique and individual mark in society and in the lives of all those he's ever touched.

He's a man of his word, also. I trust him and love him beyond words. (And it's no secret, because I'll shout that from the moun-taintops, also.) There is human love, which is so often conditioned and withheld. The love between Kirk and me is unconditional, a spiritual love and bond. I don't think he's my soul mate, I believe he's my twin flame. I believe that he and I were created simultane-ously, breathed into expression at the same moment in eternity.

Before I met Kirk, my life had been a void. Nothing physical ever filled that void. I was loved throughout my entire life, don't get me wrong, but I felt like I was a sponge and couldn't get enough. That is, until I met Kirk.

The night Kirk proposed to me, he said, "Until I met you, I thought that love was something that Hallmark created just to make money." I felt the same way.

A person in a large audience once asked me, "You give to so many people, how do you recharge?" In all honesty and without taking thought, I responded, "I go home to Kirk and after ten min-utes of being in his arms and feeling his strength, warmth, gentle-ness, and love, I am refilled to overflowing to continue to give."

To the world at large, hear me now: God is my source and strength. He just happens to pour that unlimited, pure love through a man named Kirk, who's cloaked in bodily form, allowing that purity to be rechanneled to me and everyone I touch. I don't drain Kirk any more than you drain me. He loves me, like I love you. It comes naturally without effort.

A highly religious man who works with Kirk once asked him, "What is it that your wife *really* does?" He responded, "You're a family man. You know how it is when one of your kids gets sick and how badly you wish you could take the pain, rather than allowing them to feel it?" The man replied, "Yes." Kirk said, "Well, the way you love your children and the way I love mine, Gloria just loves everyone. She's able to turn it on at will and nurture everyone the way we nurture our offspring." I was touched.

So many people, after hearing about my spiritual relationship with Kirk, tell me that they want what I've got. Never wish for what another has, wish for something like it. Never seek for love, but be open and receptive, allowing that which already lies within you to flow into the outer world of form to find you.

When I was leaving my first marriage, I wasn't looking for another relationship. Even if I had sat down, with pen in hand, and written down everything I thought I would want in a man, I would have never been able to visualize all that Kirk is to me. For the last fifteen years, since I spiritually awakened, I put everything into God's hands to take care of, reserving my personal relationship to carry on my own. There was a part of me that feared that if I put something so earthy into God's hands, He would screw it up.

If you're reserving a part of your life, thinking you have it under control, holding back from allowing that divine spirit within you to plan and handle the details, you're living the human/hard way, going without and not living up to your full potential. You don't have to sacrifice your desires and dreams. By putting them in His hands, you will find each and every one of them manifesting in your physical world, but without all the obstacles that you, as a human, must surmount and overcome. Details are handled effortlessly and easily once you allow Him to use you, instead of you trying to use Him.

Have you not noticed? Man has always prayed to God concerning the weather, praying for rain or praying to stop the rain, praying for disease to be healed or lack of money to be overcome. Why aren't the prayers answered? Are you not asking right? Are you not worthy? Are you such a bad person that you deserve this misery? I think not.

Man has sought the missing link for centuries. Perhaps some mystical groups or religions held the answers, but it was a secret and reserved for only the elite (who deserved to know). Man has been held captive by fear (false power) and ignorance.

Well, until now, when you find out that I can't keep a secret and that I'm going to tell you everything I know to help make your life brighter, healthier, richer, and more fulfilling. If God didn't want me to share, He would have never called upon me to be a messenger. I'm just doing my job, what can I say?

CHAPTER 19

I just want to hear your voice,
see your face,
and feel your touch

Gosh, it feels so good to be back in the house. Though our wood-burning stove might not be very attractive, it sure makes my life more comfortable! When I first moved to Montana, I complained about the weather, and Kirk bought me a pair of long underfudgies. I told him, "Take a good look . . . because you aren't going to see me again until the spring thaw!"

I have something I'd like to share with you, something I wrote many years ago to my friend, Nikki. After you read it, I'd like to discuss it a bit with you.

Dearest Nikki,

Greetings and good morning, my friend! This is going to probably be the last letter you ever get from me (under these circumstances). I hadn't sent you a Christmas card yet, just the insert for this year's mail-outs and I was starting to get stressed because I hadn't done that yet.

I made it my priority today to get your card in the mail, but to do that, I had to go buy it first. It had to be special; it had to say all I wanted it to say. I went to the drugstore here in town because it has the best selection. I started reading

the different cards and found myself bawling in the aisle of
the card section.

The cards were pretty, some were sentimental, some were
funny, but none seemed to say what I really wanted to say.
(Sometimes if you want something done right, ya just gotta
do it yourself, ya know what I mean?)

Just thinking about what's about to fall out of my head
onto paper gets me choked up and weepy.

Remember when I said that we had one more letter to
write to each other, to close this part of our life together (as
well as the ending for *Between Saint and Sinner*)? Well, I had
asked for your hopes and dreams and fears.

*My only hope has been to hear your voice, see your smile, and
feel your touch.*

All those things that most people take for granted in
friends or family we've been denied since the beginning of
our relationship. Once that hope is fulfilled (and it soon will
be) the rest of our lives together, the dreams unfolding and
becoming reality, and all the books and creations, that's all
just frosting on the cake!

Nikki, I adore you! Trying to say how much will never be
accomplished through the written word, but in actions as
you live with me (and the family) and experience it all firsthand.

One more thing, I just got the completed song (for Kirk's
Christmas) with all the background music in it. It turned
out beautiful. Rhonda Jean sings so beautifully, I can hardly
believe that we've pulled this off in three months. I feel so
honored to have been part of this creation. I wrote the
words, and just watching as each phase of it unfolded has
amazed me.

If I'd had more time to think about all of it, it might have
slowed the process down, filled me with fears or uncertain-
ties that I couldn't do this. But, today, held in my possession
is the completed demo tape that is so beautiful and profes-
sionally done.

Rhonda confided in me, in the past two weeks, that the

first time she met me and heard me talk about you, she felt envy. She silently raged, wishing that she'd had someone in her life like me, just someone to believe in her and support her.

She said that she had also prayed, "God, I'd love to be a friend to Gloria. I'd love her to be a part of my life."

She never confessed those feelings until we were already underway with this project. Another's dreams and prayers have been answered. I'm so impressed.

Rhonda and the world are hungry for love. They want so much to be genuinely loved by someone. I used to fear that I'd never be able to touch enough people in this lifetime (and you scolded me so long ago that even the Master could only teach twelve all He knew).

My point in adding the Rhonda story this morning was to say that just in passing, she and I met, and in a brief three-month period, we were able to pull off a completed, beautiful song for Kirk (and the world). There was no investment in friendship or learning about each other, it was a brief encounter that changed her life and that of many who will hear the story or song.

You and I have invested six years of our friendship, time, energy, tears, and triumphs. (God, I love that word!) Most people I share our story with are touched by the miracle of love that brought and holds us together. A few are fearful of your past being repeated, and a few more are fearful that you won't want to go the distance throughout the future with me. Until this morning, I'd always try to put aside the fears of others by saying that if I only had you in Montana for a short time and we were able to work together across the miles thereafter, that none of that would matter. All that would truly be important is that you stepped across the threshold and attempted the new life.

Now, I can honestly answer them from my heart without so many words. My only hope is to hear your voice, to see your smile, and to feel your touch. A treasured gift I'll *never* (again) take for granted.

Merry Christmas, my friend, with all my heart—I love you now and always will.

> Always,
> Gloria

P.S. Your first meeting with your parole officer, Sally, is January 22 at 10:30 A.M. She has already given permission for you to leave the state, to fly the friendly skies with me throughout February. All necessary paperwork will be filled out at our first meeting. See you soon. I will look forward to your call on the first. Happy New Year! Hell, we're going to give a new meaning to those words!

I may have been in denial about what to expect when Nikki was paroled to my home in Montana, but I truly didn't think I was. Kirk tried to share with me how difficult it might be, having another person demanding my time, or trying to help her feel comfortable in our home. I tried to explain to concerned family members (on both sides) and friends that Nikki *was already a part of my everyday life*. I had lived my life and sent countless letters to the prison for her to see life through my eyes.

Every vacation or promotional trip I took, I was experiencing it and writing of it immediately when I got home so that Nikki could share all I had seen and done. Each meal I set at this table had an invisible place setting for Nikki. When shopping, I always had her, in spirit, at my side. On holidays, she was with me. When she was scared, disappointed, or frightened, I projected my energies so that I could hold her. (She's pretty good at doing the same thing.)

Our biggest anxiety was always the lag in mail time and the obstacles of attempting to provide artwork and not having the correct tools with which to work. The frustrations paid off, the dedication that we showed in never giving up was a miracle in itself.

My concern was that when Nikki was paroled, others (not she, herself) would continue to see the person she used to be. The woman deserves respect and I would demand that she received nothing less than that.

Years ago, in the beginning stages of our friendship, I hadn't

heard from her for over two weeks. That was unlike her and it concerned me. I couldn't quiet myself to see with my spiritual vision or
tap in and this only served to compound my fears. I called the
prison and asked to speak to her counselor. I explained the situation and asked him to have her call me.

He was appalled that someone would think he was a secretary
to an inmate. He told me that he would pass the message on this
one time, but to never expect this again. Nikki laughed about it,
but my concerns were for all those people on the outside who don't
receive letters (or collect telephone calls) from their loved ones,
most often due to the inmates not having even a stamp, that connection to the outside world.

Nikki never did without stamps after that. They were sent, on
time at the first of every month, not even so much for her to be
able to write to me, but to reach out and touch others so that they
need not worry or concern themselves with her safety or well
being.

There are times that family or friends have taken me for granted,
or I them, mostly it is unmeaning and unintentional, but nevertheless it happens at times. We get so busy and caught up with the
world's events and all that must be done that we tend to neglect
those who are nearest and dearest to us.

I had the pleasure of going to prison twice to meet Nikki. I cried
each time I had to leave her there. I live in Montana, but my heart
was in bondage, right along with Nikki, for six years. It's not because I'm a poet or even a softie that I feel such strong feelings for
this woman. I wish you had met me a decade ago—you would
question if I was even the same person.

Just as much as I gave to Nikki, in donations of stamps, quar-
terly boxes, support, or friendship, the woman gave above and beyond beautiful drawings for my books. There are three people in
this world who know who Gloria is, inside and out. My ex–
mother-in-law, Kirk, and my friend, Nikki. Others only know what
I've allowed them to see.

Showing all of Gloria was never that easy until I became friends
with Nikki. I allow people to hear my potty mouth, which erupts at
times. I've shared my shadows with strangers to ease their guilt,

and, believe it or not, I was more afraid to tell people that I was a spiritual healer because I detested being seen as "holy." I'm just like you. Temporarily, I might leak a little more love, but I'm still overcoming my insecurities and fears, also.

There are a few highlights in my life, above and beyond seeing all the miracles that manifest through healings that I get to be part of. My children's births, my marriage to Kirk, the day I met Nikki in 1990 through the written word, the two days I "got to go to prison," the day my first book came off the press, the first time I ever saw my spiritual teacher, the night I had my Oneness Ceremony, and I guess there are quite a few others. But one of my all-time favorite highlights was the moment I realized and accepted how to find total, quiet peace in my mind and the knowingness of what that peace had to offer.

It's easy for me to feel grateful, I have a wonderful life. I didn't always have a wonderful life, though and it was when it was at its worst that I began giving thanks for every single thing I could think of.

Long ago, I heard a story about two sisters who were held in a concentration camp. The room they were held in was full of fleas. One sister complained daily and the other sister continued to beg her sister to give thanks for all things. The first sister found it difficult to do so and had no understanding of why, but she did as her sister asked.

The Nazi guards had been going to other bungalows and raping the women, but because they knew that the sisters' hut was flea-bitten, they wouldn't step over the threshold.

When my life was at its worst, I gave thanks daily, beginning with the sun rising and shining its warmth and beauty into my life, and I ended each day, giving thanks that the stars were given to Light my way in the darkest hours.

Please don't take your individual lives for granted. You trust that the sun will rise and shine its warmth and beauty in your life. You trust that the stars won't fall from the sky and will continue to light your way. You may believe that the Heavens are in divine order and your individual, personal lives aren't. That just isn't true. Remember the source from which all life springs forth. Begin to see the life that animates all things—the blades of grass, the trees, your beloved pets, your family members.

I give thanks that a convict/ex–heroin junkie touched my life with love. I give thanks for all things great and small. Take a moment daily to give thanks for all things and appreciate the beauty of life, the beauty of you.

CHAPTER 20

I'm not pure electricity yet—
Kirk thinks I'm just "static"

I really appreciate that Kirk has been helping the kids with their homework and even loaded the dishwasher for me tonight. You may be thinking that I have been neglecting the family today, spending so much time with you, but they're in good hands and have more than enough love.

Kirk teases me at times that I'm like a thunderstorm with all the energy I have and that if I only gave to the family, I'd flood them. We watched a movie together, called *Powder*, about a guy who ascended into pure energy. I asked Kirk if he thought I was getting close to that stage of being purified (becoming pure electricity), and after he finished laughing, he said, "Nope! You're just *static*!" (What a smart aleck.)

Danielle once saved her money and purchased a gift for me at a yard sale. It was a plaque for a mother. I keep it in my kitchen where I can see it daily. Here, why don't you read it for yourself?

To a Special Mom

You never let a day go by,
Without some special deed,

That brings a smile to someone's face,
Or fills a certain need.

You prove yourself a friend,
In many different ways,
And you take time to show you care.
Throughout your busy days.

For you are everything that's good,
You're everything that's kind,
And moms as wonderful as you,
Are truly hard to find.

My family comes first and that's the way it has to be. Family is the foundation of spiritual activity in a person's life. Most people are aware that I am available from 8:00 A.M. to 5:00 P.M., respecting that at 5:00, my roles as a mother and wife become more prominent. Not all emergencies occur between those hours, and there are times when my telephone rings late at night. However, for the most part, the world respects my life.

Though I don't normally see people after hours, or attend group functions or meetings, I support others by going into the Light as needed. I am extremely sensitive and highly telepathic, I've already told you about that.

I have to share a funny story about Kirk and me. (Sorry, Kirk.) I am very modest, even in front of him. On his nightstand, he has a touch lamp and each night we go through this teasing ceremony of me begging him to turn off the light so I can get into bed without being seen.

One night, I was already in bed and, all of a sudden, I grabbed the covers tightly, almost in a white-knuckled grip, and I pulled the blankets to my throat, holding them securely. In a very loving tone, Kirk asked, "What's the matter, hon?" With a wrinkled brow, I responded, "I don't know, Kirk. I just had a thought that you were going to reach over me, pretending like you were going to hug me, but then you were going to grab the covers and rip them back, exposing me." He laughed and affirmed, "That was exactly what I was going to do."

(Now do you believe me? You can lie to others, you can lie to yourself, but you can't lie to me because I know what you're going to do before you ever do it.)

Do your ears ring? Mine do and it has nothing to do with any weird medical condition. When my left ear rings, it's my soul sending me a message and its tone and frequency mean to pay attention, to beware or to be aware. The ring also tells me when divinity is about to manifest perfection in the outer world. Expect a miracle!

When my right ear rings, it's letting me know consciously that someone long distance, across the miles is seeking a healing. This I learned, like everything else, through experience.

One noon, I was sitting at my kitchen counter getting ready to eat lunch. My right ear started ringing so loudly that it was hurting me and just about knocked me off my stool. When the ringing subsided, I had a clear picture of my friend Dolores in my mind.

She felt so close, I was sure that she was going to pull up into my driveway any minute, so I left my lunch on the counter and went outside to stand at the curb. Minutes passed and she didn't arrive, so I returned to the kitchen.

Dolores should have been at work, but I could feel her presence. I called her at the shop where she was a retail clerk and was surprised when she answered the telephone. I said, "Dolores, the weirdest thing just happened to me," and after I explained the situation, she started laughing.

I, personally, didn't think it was so funny. In fact, as her laughter continued, I started to get angry and I responded, "Dolores, it wasn't funny, it really hurt my ear!" She answered me, "Oh yes it is funny. Wait till you hear what I did."

She said that, exactly at noon, the UPS truck pulled up and left an extra-large shipment, which needed to be inventoried and priced that day. Feeling overwhelmed, after the delivery man left, she literally screamed, "Gloria, I need help now!" Still laughing, she said, "If I'd have known how sensitive you were, I would have merely thought or whispered it."

Over the last ten years, my tones continue to ring day and night with people needing help. If I've already met you, when you think about me, I get a clear picture of you in my mind and I go into the Light and begin the healing process.

Unless I'm driving, when I hear a tone in my right ear, I close my eyes and go within, reaching out to that Light to dissolve the fear in whoever is reaching out to God. Even if you and I are sitting here, in deep conversation, and I get an inner tone, I will have to proceed with the healing if anyone calls.

Excuse me for a minute while I go tell D.W. and Danielle to get off the computer and off the phone. Ten o'clock is their bedtime. (Mine, too.) However, even though I go to bed so early, I use that time to do long distance healing. I've found that our kids are seldom sick because they eat right, play hard, and get plenty of rest. Living under Benish law and karmic law is the best way we Benishes experience health. When the kids go beyond their limits and preventive maintenance isn't enough, it's time for Mom to step in.

CHAPTER 21

All-knowing . . . not a know-it-all

I've had so many people ask me about fearful visions they have. Can we alter them? My answer is, *"yes."* Many prophets predicted cataclysmic events beginning with Nostradamus, and even the modern-day prophets predict doom and gloom. (I wrote a book, *The Positive Prophet*, because there are beautiful events forthcoming for man. It yet hasn't gone to print, so please just be patient.) No prophecy of destruction needs to occur if man stops putting energy into the destruction and heals the mind.

I had a friend, long ago, who was excited about the earth changes that she'd heard and read of. One evening I scolded her by saying, "You have not raised your consciousness to the point that you can manifest direct from universal God substance, so I imagine you'd be one of the first bitching and moaning that you're hungry or cold. Rather than putting energy into creating destruction, perhaps you should meditate more and raise your awareness to heal those events from ever occurring."

Another thing, those who promote fear and destruction will see it within their individual, personal worlds first. Karmic law is not a respecter of persons. If you are thinking you will be safe, but all those unenlightened souls won't be, guess again. You are the creator of your individual experiences and what you project and judge, you will experience.

One morning, while dressing, I had a vision of my daughter, Danielle (then age three) falling into the deep end of my friend's swimming pool. My friend Paula and I had been known to sit around in her backyard, not fully paying complete attention to my two toddlers. We had even been forewarned and scolded by her boyfriend and my first husband.

(It's another belief of mine that if I *hear* a prewarning or suggestion from others aloud, three times within seventy-two hours, it's a message from spirit and I'd better pay attention.)

The day I had the vision of Danielle drowning, I was getting ready to join Paula at her house for lunch. When I arrived, she answered the door and was in a bathing suit. I said, "Good, you're in a suit! Danielle's going to fall into the deep end of your pool today and you get to be the one to save her life."

We had lunch, the kids were playing, and Paula and I got deeply involved in a metaphysical discussion. In the background, I heard a noise like a small pebble falling into Paula's pool. Had I not been shown earlier that Danielle would fall into the pool, I would have ignored the sound.

Without interrupting the conversation, I said, "Paula, Danielle just fell in your pool—go get her." Lying face-down in the deep end, was Danielle.

We can change events. Nothing is written in stone and the world doesn't need to experience cataclysms in order to spiritually grow. Planet earth is becoming a spiritual planet. That was written long ago, but how it occurs is up to each of us!

Again, I'm all-knowing, not a know-it-all. Sometimes I just know things and usually, I don't tell. (You really think, like Kirk, that I can't keep a secret?) It does depend upon what it is that I know.

I have done healings on people who had cancer and they didn't know they had it. I had a choice: to heal it or to project fear, planting a possible seed to re-create it (by telling them). Since I can see and sense on a subtle level, I just erase it before it ever becomes a part of their reality.

What gives me the right to heal? What gives others the right to be sick? Am I playing God? No, I believe He's "playing" me. Disease is a result of believing in disease. It's an illusion—a mental projection of the mass consciousness of which we are a part. Mind *is* over matter and becomes physical, but if the error is erased in mind and never becomes a projection in the physical, then only good has been done.

Look at it this way: if there's only one mind, and by healing you, I'm healing my own consciousness, I have ever right, don't I? As do you!

One afternoon, I was called upon to heal a baby. He was tired and kept pushing my hands away. When I returned home, I told Kirk that I knew that the baby was going to die if I couldn't help him. The parents didn't know that the child had been born with a heart defect and it wasn't something that I wanted to share with them. I could see it and knew, as well, that the lungs had not fully developed. The child was, indeed, very ill. Far sicker than the parents knew.

As a human, I was torn up about it. There was no way I could tell the parents, not even to make them aware so they could take the child to the doctor for X-rays. The X-rays and doctors weren't going to be able to do anything anyway. This diagnosis wasn't something I was just assuming, it was what was being shared from within.

I could attempt to work on the child long distance, but I really felt this was something I needed to do in person. Sometimes that happens. I could receive fifteen calls in one day, and I could tell people not to come to me because I can help them from a distance. But the sixteenth call could be the one in which I know they should get on a plane to come see me. I await spirit's decision as to who should come, and who can receive love across the miles.

That day, I turned it over to God I offered myself to be used in whatever way was necessary to help this child.

Two days later, the child was brought to me. The parents lay him on my bed, fast asleep, and I rubbed my hands together and placed them on his chest. I felt a powerful burst of energy as his head and lungs were restored to normal, and I knew the child would live a wonderful life.

Not being a doctor, I can't diagnose illness—nor can you, nor would I want to. Any disease is the result of an erroneous belief system. Disease is just the effect. Belief is the cause of any and all outer disturbances, physically, financially, morally, mentally, or spiritually.

I was being invited to a church, as guest speaker for services. I would be traveling a long distance to do so and before I ever left my home, I meditated (to be given the speech as well as the energy to deliver it). Following the brief meditation, I felt approximately twenty electrical charges. The power surges filled me with all the energy I would need.

I was in awe, myself, that I was given so much Light, which I would carry with me. This was a first experience such as this. What it told me was that I was going to be sharing that Light with a whole lot of people.

I arrived at the church, spoke as a guest for a course in miracles group later that day, and was invited to stay to teach a healing workshop. Up until that time, I had only taught ten to fifteen people in a workshop. I had stepped outside the church to take a break, and was asked several times to come inside and teach the workshop. I continued to remain outside in the quiet, stating that I would be in shortly. I just needed the break.

When I walked into the church, I was met by 120 people who wanted to learn to do what I do. I was in shock. I wasn't sure if I was prepared for this type of a turnout. I taught the workshop, however, and at the end, I asked those who wanted a healing hug to line up. One at a time, I hugged 120 people that afternoon.

The last person seeking a healing was a forty-eight-year-old woman who had been born with a paralyzed arm, after a doctor used forceps during her birth. Her right hand was in a fist and her arm hung lifelessly at her side.

I sat her on the floor, placing my hands on top of her head, closed my eyes, and allowed the Light to enter my consciousness. She had several electric shocks that literally lifted her off the floor and she cried out, "Oh, my God, what's happening to me?" I quietly whispered in her ear that she was safe.

I could see "my Boss" standing before us (and I always feel pretty dad-gummed secure in those moments). He telepathically told me to have the woman open her palm. She said she couldn't. He nodded His head and I repeated what I heard from within. He said, "You can." She opened her fingers until it exposed an open palm.

He shared a second message and I asked her to raise her right arm. As before, she shook her head, stating, "I can't do that, I've never been able to do that." Again, He nodded His head and I repeated the inner message, "Well, you can now." She raised her right arm above her head, laughing and crying simultaneously.

I share this story now because of the many times that we (yes, you and me) say "I can't." When we say "can't," we stop and block the flow of energy. We can, in fact, we can do it easy. Notice how many times you limit that power within you from doing the greater works. (Perhaps humanly, we can't—but God is the one doing it—so don't limit Him!)

When divine guidance told me so long ago not to idolize Him, but to raise my conscious awareness and just do it, I had to ponder all that could occur if I was to do so. In the Bible, He said, "These and greater works ye can do." I'm demonstrating the truth of those words, through my consciousness of God, and so can you.

Years ago, I sat looking at my reflection in the smoked-glass mirror of a walnut lamp next to my recliner. I had been reading a spiritual book and my awareness was expanded. I felt at peace with the world and myself in that moment. In my thoughts, I affirmed, Light shines through every single pore of my being.

A cloudy, milky-white energy formed around me and my reflection disappeared out of the mirror. I didn't disappear, just my reflection. I thought it was awesome though, so I ran down to my bathroom mirror and repeated the same thing. Silently, I affirmed again, Light shines through every single pore of my being. As before, the cloudy, milky-white energy surrounded me and my reflection disappeared from the bathroom mirror.

I practiced in public, I taunted my kids by disappearing in the house and they couldn't find me. (Talk about the new version of hide and seek.) This gift wasn't given to me to perform or do tricks. I had become aware of my true, spiritual nature, which is pure consciousness, appearing as form/physical being. Later, I found that in walking among the masses this gift could be used for my protection.

Because I am so telepathic, if someone is thinking of doing harm to me, I can raise my vibration and disappear. You are going to be experiencing a heightening or quickening of spirit in the future days to come. Each time you go into the Light, your telepathy is going to be fine-tuned. You are also going to become extremely sensitive (and perhaps receive tones). All that I am sharing herein will begin occurring for you, also. (I believe that everyone who finds their way to this book is already experiencing most of what I have shared and you're receiving valid answers. For others, it will give you an awareness of all that is a part of your future.) I, at present, must be a forerunner or something, because I know that I'm supposed to share these things that have occurred.

Not to set me apart or separate me from you, as being special. I am not special, I can do this and so can you.

One evening, in a dream, I was sitting Indian-style across from a man. He held out his hands to me very lovingly. I placed my hands in his and, the moment I did, he grabbed my wrists and held them tightly. It scared me and as I was trying to pull back from him, he tightened his hold on me.

In the dream, I saw my heart center open fully and a beautiful, brilliant white cylinder of Light went from my heart to the man's heart, and as it touched him, it blew him away. As I awakened, I was still in awe of what I'd been shown. I wondered what the dream meant.

I was in Arizona, speaking before a group of women. The husband of one of the women entered the room and from across the room, I could feel his anger, hate, and darkness. (He was also well known, in the area, for performing black magic.)

I remembered my dream, opened my heart, smiled at him, and sent a beautiful cylinder of white Light to his heart center. The moment I saw the Light touch his heart, in my mind, he jumped up and ran out the door.

Because this happened so fast and without any effort, I briefly thought, Maybe he left his lights on. However, we all then heard him burning rubber as he sped away from the house. The women looked at me and questioned, "What was that all about?"

I was still, to some extent, disbelieving that what I'd done had anything to do with the outer experience. I was honest with them. I told them what I felt and sensed from his presence concerning me. I shared what I had visualized, explaining that they had seen the end result. (I concluded with an authoritative whisper, "This shit really works.")

My love Light isn't meant to harm. It will, however, mirror a person's hatred if they are not willing to have their ugliness or fear dissolved in the Light.

The woman who was married to this man saw me briefly the next day. She said, "When I got home last night, my husband said, 'You're not allowed to play with Gloria anymore, she's a witch!' She continued, "I just responded, 'Honey, she just mirrored your crap right back in your face!'"

The Light is your protection, it's who you really are. You know how we're all taught that we, as humans, only use about 10 percent of our brain? As you continue having your quiet time, allowing the violet Light to flow into your mind, it is expanding. All those things you imagine you can do, you can do. You will be shown, as I have been, how each new talent fits into what He is asking you to do.

I'm not here to do tricks. I was speaking with a woman once and she asked me if I would disappear for her. I wasn't trying to, but during our discussion of mystical events that occur through me, she replied, "Hey, it must be my imagination. It looks like you're starting to fade out." I lit a cigarette and as I was inhaling (it lowered my energy), and she said, "Yeah, it was just my imagination. You're still all here."

Under karmic law, drinking, drugs, and cigarettes all lower a soul's energy field. Of themselves, they have no power, only the power given to them by an individual's belief systems. Normally, I don't drink, but one afternoon a friend came by and we shared a few beers. One would have toasted me, but I happened to have two that day so I was pretty well loaded.

I'm sharing this experience because I believe it's important for you to know. That afternoon, in the woman's presence and while awaiting my husband to come home from work, I had the thought to put six to eight quartz crystals in a glass bowl with equal amounts of apple cider vinegar and sea salt. I did as my thoughts requested and covered the crystals with water.

I was then guided to place my hands in the water and *within* moments, I was completely sober. I was cleansed and detoxified. The crystals magnified the cleansing process. If I hadn't experienced it, I might not have believed it.

I'm not promoting crystals or the sales for them and I'm not asking you to run out and buy crystals, sea salt, or vinegar to perform this ritual. Everything in a crystal is in you. Some people need tools and this is appropriate, but I'm telling you also, that you don't need the tools. It gives you awareness, but it also teaches you that you can do this same thing, without the need of purchasing anything. The Light in you cleanses your mind, purifying the false beliefs, and will appear outwardly as healing and higher energy.

I'm a physical person, enjoying the pleasures of a physical planet. I have no judgments against alcohol, drugs, cigarettes, food, entertainment, or anything of an effect. I have a good time, I enjoy my life, I live in balance, and allow spirit to guide me through every single moment.

Just for a quick example, I'll explain why I don't have human judgment concerning physical things. Let's take a rose into our thoughts. Is a rose, of itself, good or bad? For those who love flowers or the essence of a beautiful rose, they may judge it as good. However, someone with hay fever may judge that same rose as bad. Each individual's perception, giving a rose the power for good or bad, determines their judgment for or against it.

A rose is a rose. A cigarette is a cigarette. Judgments that say cigarettes are bad tell us that cigarettes cause cancer, emphysema, and a variety of other illnesses. However, judgments that say cigarettes are good point to their reducing tension and stress, alleviating the need to eat, etc. Heal both judgments and you will also see that a cigarette is just a cigarette, with no power in itself. Alcohol, without judgment, guilt, and fear is just alcohol. The only power that something in our outer world has comes from within our judgments. On the path to enlightenment some of the "things" that you've been doing, at present, may fall away peacefully as you open yourself to carry more Light. As each judgment is healed, your experiences will change.

I have not yet walked on water or through walls. I'm not a saint and I don't want to be one. I'm a messenger. God doesn't want you to be another Gloria running around (Lord, I don't think the world could handle that anyway). He wants you to be you, He wants you to learn discernment, He wants you to enjoy your life, He gives you every opportunity to know love, direct.

Please, don't put me on a pedestal, because you would just come along and knock me off later anyway. I will not allow it. If you believe me to be special now, you would feel anger later when you discover that I'm just the norm of this golden age. It may appear that I'm further along on the path. As a teacher, explaining the process simply, I need to be more advanced. That doesn't make me special as a teacher. It just makes me a teacher. Once students have learned and demonstrated that knowledge, they are not special either. It just means that they have acquired the same knowledge and awareness. My purpose is not to nag, threaten, frighten, or shame you. My purpose is to teach, forgive, and love.

Your smoking, drinking, cussing, etc., does not keep you from being a spiritual/human being and God isn't angry if you are doing any of it. God is purity and love that you can only now begin to imagine, but you will be touched by it and your life will be transformed. You, as a human, don't have the power to make that revelation occur, so you might as well stop berating yourself and others regarding it. It will happen when it's meant to happen. It only requires an openness on your part.

God is the master gardner, planting the seed of desire for a spiritual life in your heart. Your desires aren't separate from His. (Personally, I used to gag if people tried to cram God down my throat.) Once I was touched and called by spirit, it became all that mattered.

If you, or your loved ones aren't seeing eye to eye with your spiritual beliefs or your desires to have them healed, they deserve to be left alone, and receive their own calling, without your static or controlling. No human can drag another to the Light. Honor and respect one another's religions and beliefs. (Heal your perception and judgments concerning them, and they just might get the healing you were desiring for them.)

Let me tell you a little more about the electric shocks that I keep talking about. It literally feels like I've been shocked by an electrical appliance or outlet, except it hurts good, if that makes any sense.

The Bible says that God is omnipresent, which means that He's everywhere. Spiritual books that have been written also confirm this theory. Even though God, like electricity, *is* present everywhere, if you don't plug into it, it's not going to bring you Light, warmth, or any of the other things that God/electricity can do. Just having an intellectually bright idea about the words won't accomplish anything—you must individually plug in.

When you plug a 110-volt human personality into 220-volt divine mind, you make the ultimate connection to the source. In reality, there is only one mind and we are individual aspects of the one mind, but so that we can understand it easier, I'm using this analogy.

Once the belief is purified from mind, however, a shift in consciousness occurs and can be physically felt; a shift in perception has occurred and a miracle will appear outwardly. When I feel the electrical shift, I know that the Christ is on the scene and my part is complete. I then experience the peace that passeth all human understanding. Ha! And Kirk thinks I'm just static. Well, I'll tell you what—it's okay if you're a little overwhelmed with all the miracles I share, because personally speaking, I'm a little shocked, myself.

Now let me make you a Turtle sundae? Wonder what that is? Well, I put two large scoops of vanilla ice cream into a bowl, and generously pour caramel topping on one scoop and delicious hot fudge on the other. Even more generous portions of whipped cream follow, with at least three or four whole pecans. All this is topped with a juicy cherry.

Would you like a small or large sundae, sweetie?

CHAPTER 22

Healing the child within

It's time for me to say goodnight to the kids, so I'd like you to take a few minutes with Kirk to chat or to sit quietly and think about some of the things I've shared with you today. I make it a point, on most every night to sit or lie with Danielle, listening to her angers or concerns of the day. I give all of my kids and loved ones the permission to share their hate, anxiety, or fears.

Even at age sixteen, Danielle still likes that quiet time of me lying with her, doing "energy work," healing her pains after a night of sports. When I was a child, I would have loved to have this awareness and to receive a safe place to dissolve my fears or erase my hidden pains. Unfortunately, most of us never had that luxury of nurturing attention.

I'm not placing blame. I'll explain more of that when I return. It should be about twenty minutes and I'll be back.

Thanks for your patience! Sometimes God's so smart it amazes me. Every single moment of our lives is so incredible once we learn to listen to all the signals and symbols that are going on around us.

Tonight, Danielle asked me why I used to bite my fingernails and how I stopped. Danielle is still a master teacher for me. God knew what He was doing when her soul chose to incarnate as a part of my life. I answered her direct. I explained I bit my nails because I had been a nervous person in my youth. She questioned me again, wanting to know what made me nervous, and I found myself sharing that I was afraid of everyone and everything. Innocently, she asked why I was afraid of everyone and everything, and it made me think about it.

I was able to share freely. She gave me that same security I give her. So much healing continues for me, I've already told you that my life is an open book. I've teasingly told others that I share every aspect of my life, through the written word, and that I write books for adult children, so they can heal their dysfunctions. But, that because my life was so dysfunctional, it would give me a lifetime of material.

I figure that if I'm honest with the world, God, and myself then I have no secrets that will come back to haunt me or bite me in the behind later. If I ever became popular, it would be difficult for media to sensationalize me or make any money off sales. The world is being told firsthand of my experiences and as I become aware of my issues, I'm going to be the first one to talk about them. (Maybe that's what my friend Nikki meant when she said "that I would be great on stage because I'm not afraid to make an ass of myself"? Because—sometimes I am an ass!)

If I have an issue and don't share, it's only because I'm not totally aware of it, yet. It's my policy to always be honest with you and to be consistent so that I have a trust built within you to feel safe enough, to be who you are.

Since we have now arrived at that point in our friendship, I want you to be aware of what happens with people when they come to me for a healing or what may occur when someone comes to you for help. In the beginning of my spiritual growth, I was able to tap into the source and allow spirit to speak whatever that person needed to hear to heal their problems and pain. I was more interested, at that time, in helping others because it left no time for me to come out of denial and accept that I also had problems. The attention on others left no time for me.

Many of the patterns and pain in adult children are a result of their childhood experiences. There are countless books and programs available nowadays "to heal the child within." The methods are appropriate, but I don't believe that it takes years of therapy to heal the child within. It, of course, takes a willingness to recall that pain and to feel it, and once you have the awareness, the processing and healing is complete.

I won't lie to you. (I spent a lifetime of lying to myself.) I've said this before, but I must say it again—when you place your hands on the heart center of another or on yourself, it can be very painful. But, if you can feel it, you can heal it. In remembering my healing of the child within, I'm going to share a poem that just fell out of my head earlier this morning before you arrived.

Cryin' in the Rain

As I take a lonely walk down memory lane,
I find myself feeling a deep and ancient pain.
A pain that hurts as it did back then,
An emotional scar that proves where I've been.

Leaves crackle beneath my feet, my steps taking me back in time,
I watch my thoughts, as an observer, acting out in mime.
For no words, at this moment, could express the sadness I feel,
Just a knowingness within that it's a part of me to heal.

Tears flow down my cheeks—or is it a summer rain?
Cleansing my heart, mind, and soul, dissolving all my pain.
A child lives within me, a child who's been hurt and denied,
A child who was promised love and truth and found "that they had
lied."

But, with a smile on my face, I lied to me . . .
Telling others, "It's okay" if that's who they had to be.
I denied my hurt and anger, I swallowed the poison straight.
Convincing myself I was bad, if I ever admitted to hate.

For years, I cried within, still flashing the world a smile.
Dying inside, a little more each day, pretending all the while.

My funeral was held a few days ago, they buried the old me.
I believe in resurrection and rebirth, you too will surely see.

For, I stand before you, as a master, reborn as a child of the Light,
To live my life to the fullest and to do what I know to be right.
To love those who've hurt me, to forget and to forgive,
Enjoying each and every moment for as long as I shall live.

My child within has healed as I was cryin' in the rain,
Unaware I wasn't alone while walking down memory lane.
He whispered, "My child, I'm closer to you than hands or breath,
You're never apart from me, whether it's in life, sleep or death.

"It only seemed We were separate for a moment in human time,
It was one of the chapters you wrote, while acting out in mime.
We are truly one, that's how it will forever be,
You found the truth, and are eternally set free.

"And now as the world sees your smile, shining ever so bright,
Within their hearts, they will see and recognize your Light.
It will erase their darkness and heal their ancient pain,
On the day they find themselves . . . walking down memory lane."

The healing of my child within began years ago, when the presence of God came to me one evening, telling me we were going through the atonement process. I, of course, had no idea what those words meant and told Him so. He told me that atonement meant forgiveness and that throughout my life, experiences had occurred where I had hurt others or they had hurt me. It was time to forgive.

My response to Him was, "Well, this shouldn't take very long, because I've been a very nice person my whole life." *Not!* As long-forgotten memories were placed in my mind, I began remembering.

Times that I had even been sarcastic were shown to me, but without judgment. All of these memories of experiences weren't being shown to me to make me feel more guilt. They were being shown, for my awareness, so that I could choose more consciously whether to continue in the same way. The process took approximately two weeks. Any moment that I was in silence, my mind was being purified.

I couldn't place blame on others or on myself, for we were all doing the best we could, within the society in which we lived. My parents had hurt me, but I also had hurt and disappointed them. At every moment, I was being shown that they were doing the best they could with the awareness they had.

I had hurt siblings, friends, and coworkers. I silently asked each to forgive me. I was also shown, of course, long-forgotten moments where others had hurt me, those times when I smiled and said, "It's okay, really, it's okay." Being tough had a high price to pay at the soul level!

My friend Nikki who once had a $600-day heroin habit, has been judged by society. My addiction (to always being nice) was socially accepted, but just as deadly. I could write an entire book just about my personal experience of healing the child within. To you, you can breathe easier because I'm not going to take you through all the boring details.

I know now, however, why I attracted alcoholics into my life (even though I didn't self-righteously drink.) I became aware why I started smoking, why people's anger frightened me, why I couldn't be honest with myself or fully honest with others.

One day, when I was just a toddler, I made my dad angry and he punished me severely. That experience went so deeply into my soul that any time I found someone angry with me, I became petrified. For self-preservation, my message to myself had become that I would do whatever it takes to make people like me.

I even lied to myself and my family that I was living a happy life. After nineteen years of marriage, I finally told my first husband, "I'm not happy and I know you're not either. I just can't pretend any longer." I walked away, feeling weak, guilty, and extremely stupid for staying so long.

I married Kirk, my eternal flame, after my divorce. He has never once complained about anything I've ever cooked. In fact, on most nights, he thanks me. He teased me that coffee should smell and

taste like coffee. What a revelation for me. I would have done better if I'd known. (Isn't that an important guilt-reducing statement
if we would merely remember it? We would all "do better" if we
had the complete awareness to do so.)

I asked him why he didn't tell me long ago that he wasn't satis-
fied with the coffee and he said, "Because I didn't want to upset
you and have you leave me." Bless his heart. What a burden he's
carried, fearing that something so trivial could make a difference
in the way I feel about him.

But, in fact, it could have, if I'm honest. I had spent nineteen
years with a man who I bragged about to others, "We never fight."
Of course we didn't fight, but we never talked either. Nineteen
years of not talking or telling him how I felt built up, until one day
I could no longer stay. I was grateful that Kirk felt safe enough to
be honest.

Two years ago, I quit smoking completely. I was tired of Danielle,
learning at school that every cigarette you smoke takes fifteen minutes off your life and hearing about it from her. Kirk also has judgments about smoking and would share his beliefs and concerns, "I
just don't want you to get cancer; believing you can heal it when it
happens. Maybe you will, and maybe you won't." I asked him to
not project his fears on me.

In place of smoking, I took up crocheting and made seven
afghans for my loved ones, calling them security blankets. I was at
peace with not smoking any longer. I was a successful nonsmoker
for more than seven months and then I began cheating. I regressed
to living a lie at home, but while promoting one of my books, the
entire world could know that I smoked.

But, it wasn't the world's approval that I wanted or even
needed. I needed Kirk and Danielle's approval. I was feeling fear of
disappointing them, though in my dreams, they knew and we discussed it openly. I asked God for peace of mind. I wasn't asking for
a healing. I had surrendered my judgment that cigarettes had a
power for good in the enjoyment of them and dissolved the fear
that they could hurt my loved ones or me.

The game ended once I realized that smoking was intercon-
nected with my fear of anger (my own or another's). If I was telling

the world that I believed in happily-ever-after fairy-tale marriages and couldn't be open and honest with my immediate family members, then it was just another lie. It's sometimes difficult to be totally honest and open to the world, sharing every secret of my life in an attempt for others to see themselves through my life. It has never been hard to speak of the spiritual side of me, talking to God, or writing about miracles. I can't justify them or prove them. I don't want to try. Those things just happen and can never be scientifically explained. The results, however, for all those people I've touched says enough.

To be truthful and show my shadows to the world takes great courage. It does take immense amounts of courage, every day of my life, depending upon what I'm being faced with. I have faith. I have all the faith in the world, in God (as I know Him to be), as well as in myself, Kirk, our relationship, and involving other people chosen to play out this life with me.

During the future days, as you heal, you will meet circumstances that sometimes overwhelm you or paralyze you with fear. Take a deep breath, close your eyes, see that pinpoint of white Light, feel His presence and know that He'll manifest as your strength.

Those moments when you're most frightened are placed there for your greater good and spiritual growth. What's the worst thing that could happen if you were honest with yourself and others? That one you'll have to answer yourself.

For me, it was that I would lose approval or be physically hurt. I no longer need the approval because, within myself, I know that because of God, I have accomplished far more in this life than I could have ever dreamed possible. I am healing and trust that I'll never be physically hurt again, because I will never again depend upon man, or earth, but only on the infinite spirit of love that flows through me.

I never smoke in my home or anyone else's home or in a car. Would you like to join me outside, under the stars while I have a cigarette?

CHAPTER 23

The Goddess of Love is love in action

Aren't the stars beautiful tonight?! I love to see Venus in the sky, glowing so brightly and sometimes being mistaken for a star. It's the planet of love, maybe that's what attracts me to it so.

I didn't tell you, but when I was born I was brought home from the hospital unnamed. My grandmother was a doctor and delivered me. I went through life singing, "Born Free"—my grandma's a doctor.

I didn't know until recently how my parents named me. My dad was reading a magazine and called out to my mother, in another part of the house, "Esther, how does *Gloria* sound?" She yelled back, "Sounds great to me!" Moments later, my dad turned the page of the magazine and hollered out to my mom once again, "How does Diane sound for a middle name?" She called back quickly, "Sounds fine to me!" As my dad continued to read the article, he learned that *Diane* symbolized The Goddess of the Moon—and protector of the home.

The word "goddess" just reminded me of a letter that my friend Nikki received from one of her dear friends in prison. Nikki shared this letter with me. I think it's important to introduce you to Cindy, so you can experience one of the many letters that Nikki

167

and I receive from others. Here, let's step over by the light coming
from the garage so I can read it to you.

Cindy had been dealing with lifelong rage issues that culmi-
nated in drug use, abusive relationships, and prison terms. She was
finally able to face the issues that created her lifestyle, just prior to
her parole.

Did I tell you what my new affirmation is? I say it several times
a day, "I will actively seek the Goddess *within* my soul and be
the woman I was created to be."

There are so many things opening up for me, especially spiritually. Perhaps it's the joy in this that makes me no longer
afraid to be alone—girlfriend, I've got two good legs that will
hold me up just fine.

Ha! I feel sort of like that commercial for the fat-free lunch-
meat, "Free—Free . . . finally free!" I'm free to do anything
now, unhampered by another's weight upon my shoulders.
Why, I can leap tall buildings—I am a woman, hear me roar!
Why, I can run through tall grass naked if I take a notion! Ha!
At forty-three if I decide to run anywhere naked, I'd better find
some real tall grass!

As soon as I get home to mom's, I'm going to put my clock
up on the wall. I'm glad I mailed it to her house. I have so little
left now. Mom was able to get my clothes, music box collec-
tion, crystals, pyramid, wizards, and metaphysical books. My ex
has a strange hold on all else, but perhaps these things are
enough. Hell, I know that last line doesn't fool you. I'm pissed
as hell about my things. Certainly there will be another life lesson dealing with these material things. I would like my pictures
back though—these include my son's childhood photos on up
through time. Many photos can't be replaced . . . brothers and
sisters, long dead and gone, etc. I don't seem to be able to let go
of these things and can't help but worry about the time I may
just lose it, anger taking over, and I'll go to take my things.

It seems like I've been working on this anger issue of mine
for so long now. I long for the lesson to be complete so I can
turn the page. Being the willful, stubborn, often hardheaded

person I am, more times than not (in fact, always) my life lessons come hard for me, but they do come.

I'm certain they would come easier if I didn't resist so. So often, it's like I dig my heals in and shout at the Universe, "Hell no, I won't go!" I know in my heart of hearts that the waters of life will carry me exactly where I need to go. So, why oh why, do I waste so much time and energy trying to swim upstream?

Along with the massive amounts of self-help books I keep my nose in, I've been made aware of many things about myself. Whenever I catch myself resisting, I actively make an attempt to feel the pain and (or whatever), experience it, learn from it, and then release it. Lord knows I've grown weary of the same old repeated lessons.

Gee, it's past time I move on to another class, get to a higher level. At this time, I truly believe that I'm ready. For years and years, I've cowardly used the drugs to cover the pain so I wouldn't have to face, do battle with, and overcome the inner issues. Yes, I said, "cowardly"—after all, these inner issues can be monsters, as you well know.

Yes, I've been clean since March 3, 1994—but in years past, I've been clean *several times*. The difference in then and now is clear to me. My view of the whole drug issue is different. Somewhere in this last couple of years, I've come to see that drugs are not the problem. A bag of dope can sit forever and not hurt you—yet they can and do kill you. I plainly see that drugs are not the problem. The problem is the inner issues that make a person want to pick up that bag in the first place. Once we begin (and continue throughout our lives) to heal ourselves from *within* then the possibility of us even desiring to use no longer exists.

To me, the greatest gift, is to become a blessing. To be able to touch the life of even one person in a profound and meaningful way. I know, with all my being, that in just such a manner . . . something very big waits for me.

You see, God requires everyone to do something. Perhaps the hard roads I have traveled were only the means to take me where I need to be.

I'll close this here and send it out with much love to you and Gloria. Take care, Sugar Bear—let me know all about your further adventures.

> Love you, love you, love you,
> Love, light and laughter,
> Cindy

I had just shared the importance of healing my inner child, and I felt so strongly that I needed to share an "outsider's" experience, also. I attempt to answer every single letter I receive, reaffirming people's feelings, attitudes, and giving them a safe place to express "all of themself." Cindy's letter affected me so strongly that the tears rolled down my face, and I relived her experiences along with her. I was saddened that the false teachings of the world could make a human suffer like this.

So many of those who surround me complain of petty, irritating situations in their lives, they are so completely immersed within themselves that they can't see how fortunate they are. It's in those moments that I'd like to personally share some of the mail I receive, so that people will look beyond themselves to others who have chosen to walk away from Oz, rather than to it. The journeys some people have taken tire me in just the retelling.

Cindy prayed, as a child, to be someone special, unaware throughout her forty-three years that she didn't have to do anything in order to be special, that she already was. When I became aware of Cindy's desire to "touch the life of even one person in a profound and meaningful way," I knew I had to share her letter with you today. She touched Nikki, she touched me, I think you'll agree her story and life, in itself, *is* touching.

Cindy's a model for you, me, and countless others. Her life and pain was not in vain. She's a remarkable woman. As Nikki shared this letter, she continued to laugh and say, "My God! I love this woman." So do I and one day, I'll have the pleasure of meeting her personally, so I can physically place my arms around this woman and thank her for touching my life with love.

CHAPTER 24

Walking my talk

It's such a beautiful night! Would you mind very much taking just one more walk around our quiet neighborhood?

One day, while I was in Boise, Idaho, teaching a healing workshop, I met a young man named Russell. He had a thirty-minute appointment scheduled for an individual healing. He had been asked, the day before I arrived, if he would like the open slot and he said he would.

I had been told about Russell the afternoon I arrived. When he was seventeen years old, he and a friend hot-wired and "borrowed" a car, a prank that ended in a disastrous accident. The friend was only mildly injured, but Russell's injuries resulted in a three-month coma, which felt like eternity to his family. When he awoke, Russell was told his motor skills were gone, and that he could not be healed medically. He was told the result of the accident would affect the rest of his life.

Lucky for me, I don't know what motor skills are. I'm not afraid of hearing a "death sentence" or the medical profession's doom-and-gloom "this is the way it is" stories. When I came face to face with Russell, I looked up at a tall, good-looking young man who was now twenty-five years old. He hadn't been told anything about me, what I do or how I do it.

His head, I might add, lay tilted to the side, his neck muscles unable to hold it straight. He could speak, with difficulty. He walked, but with a straight-legged limp.

Before I started working on him, I briefly explained that I was going to turn on soft music to relax him, and then I told him I was going to rub my hands together and place them on his head, heart, and back. I asked if he felt comfortable with me doing this, and he nodded his head yes.

I began the music, lay hands on Russell's head, and closed my eyes. Within, I could see so much black, heavy energy. However, the feeling beneath my hands started to surprise me. Under my hands, I could feel tremendous heat and pain, along with an erratic energy. Immediately, it felt like God's hands were (humanly) one with mine. The sensation of loving warmth filled me to the point that I wanted to just place my arms around this young man and nurture him, cry with him, be one with him.

When I wrote these words, I feared for a moment you might think the act is a sensual one and it isn't. It's a feeling that, if I could, I would ask a person to move over and allow me to crawl inside their skin with them. It's a spiritual closeness unlike anything in the physical realm.

Beneath my hands, I could feel the movement of energy shifting. In my mind, I was recognizing spirit reconnecting damaged areas. I watched the beautiful violet healing Light, flooding through my mind, knowing Russell was being healed on many, many levels.

When I finished twenty minutes later, I asked for the usual heart-to-heart hug. I whispered in his ear, "Russell, while I was doing the healing work and you had your eyes closed, did you see anything?" Without hesitation, he responded, "Oh yes, I watched a pretty purple color."

Russell had never been told the violet Light could be seen. He had no prereference of what I do. He, like an innocent child, was just sharing an experience. I explained what the Light does.

It was so gradual that neither Russell or I noticed, we had to be told by another bystander. His head no longer tilted to the side, it was held straight and proud. He was also speaking clearer.

I invited Russell, as my guest, to the healing workshop the following day so he would receive all the awareness to completely heal his life. He came to the workshop and I looked at him many times throughout the day. He was such an inspiration to me.

At the end of the workshop, we stood talking about our experiences. He said he knew he would be completely healed and now understood *why* he had been in the accident. Also, why we had met. He spoke of his service to God, and how he would enjoy reaching out to other kids who've been told there was no hope. Russell held a vision, like me, of giving hope to the hopeless and encouraging the discouraged. He said he would teach others how to heal their lives.

Through word of mouth, upon my return back home, I was told Russell (following the workshop) said, "I had more fun than I've ever had before in my life." (Joy is a spiritual gift that tells us we're on the right track.)

People ask me quite often if I've ever had failures. In person, on stage, when I speak of this experience, it makes me weepy. A very good friend of mine called me from Denver, telling me she had been diagnosed with lung cancer. I told her I'd begin working on her immediately, long distance.

Lee shared that if it was all the same to me, she would rather drive to Montana, to have me physically touch her. Lee and her husband arrived and I worked on her for an hour. We went for a walk afterward and we talked. I loved her so very much. The following day, I gave her a second treatment. I had seen the violet Light flooding my awareness, she felt the love, and we both felt shifts occur. Something inside me said this was something I needed to continue working on across the miles.

Two months later, I received a telephone call from Lee's daughter, telling me Lee had died that morning. I went for a walk and was gone for hours, crying and feeling that I had failed Lee. Now, I know better than to think I have the power to succeed or fail, but we all have egos. I would have felt bad enough if I had failed with a stranger to whom I had no emotional ties, but to lose a dear friend, it was almost more than I could bear.

Lee's husband, Barry, called me days later and, rather than me comforting him, he found himself giving me reassurance. Through my tears, I was asking for forgiveness for failing them. He quietly said, "Gloria, but you *did* help Lee." I asked, "My God, she died, what do you mean I helped her?"

Barry said, "Lee went into the hospital for tests. The morning before she died, the doctors saw it, Lee saw it and I saw it, the lung cancer was gone." Startled, I questioned, "But, if the lung cancer was gone, then why did she die?" Barry replied, "They were moving her from the hospital bed, to the gurney, to take her down for tests on her brain, when a tumor in her brain exploded. She died instantly."

He also explained, "Lee kept a diary of her cancer, from the day she was told, until the day she entered the hospital. She asked, if anything went wrong, she wanted you to have those writings so you could weave them into your writings to help other people." (I choke back a sob now as I share this. Excuse me while I show more of the human me. I need a hug, please.)

Lee's life and death wasn't a failure. You and I both need to be aware, we will share the Light and love with all who will accept it, but none of us can say how the healing will manifest in the outer world. For Lee, the violet Light dissolved imperfection. Since we don't see the whole plan, perhaps the next time she incarnates, she will be without some forms of human suffering she may have had to experience if she hadn't received that final touching of the spirit.

I don't have all the answers and I won't pretend I do. As a healer and as a human, I'm always doing the best I can. I'll share every moment and awareness I have attained to help make your lives better. But, please never look to me as being great and wise.

You will also find yourselves reaching out to people, to be of service, in the oddest places. As an instrument, being used, you should make it a habit to open yourself to the Light before you even leave your home to go to the grocery store. You just never know whom you might be meeting.

My parents came one summer to visit. They needed an oil change and we drove to a nearby town to get their car serviced. We were sitting in the waiting room and a woman sitting across from me was lighting a cigarette. I watched her inhale and saw adorable dimples appear on her face.

Without thinking about it, I spoke my thought aloud concerning how cute her dimples were. Her response startled me, as well as my parents, "I must be dirt-dog ugly because my boyfriend beats me all the time." Holding a section of her hair, she continued, "This is the only hair I have left, all that my boyfriend hasn't pulled out."

I began telling her who I am, what I do, and was writing out my telephone number and address in case she ever wanted to get in touch with me. For ten minutes, we talked faster than speeding bullets. I walked her to the parking lot and I held her as she sobbed in my arms.

My parents watched from the car in amazement, unaware of what had just happened through a simple statement to a stranger. As I got in the car, my mom mentioned that she couldn't believe what had just happened. I responded, "Mom, this stuff happens all the time to me. It just happens to be the first time you ever got to watch me in action."

This stranger called me several months later, leaving a message on my answering machine. She was giving God and me great praises, and told me that after our meeting, she had gotten enough courage to leave the abusive relationship. She had purchased both my books and had used them as tools to recover. She had gotten a job, and was feeling good about her life.

Thanks for this time together in the clear air. Sounds like we got back to the house at just the right time! You just heard the telephone ringing and it's nearly 9:30, but I can tell by the woman's voice on the answering machine that I need to pick it up and help. Follow me back into the house and watch how I heal people across the miles.

CHAPTER 25

Oneness

Do you remember when I shared that people would ask my mom, concerning my healing talent, "But, how does she do it?" She would answer, "Hell if I know, but it works!" The reason I'm able to be used as an instrument to heal across the miles is because I have a conscious awareness of *oneness*. In my books and the writings of others, we hear that word and it sounds poetic, but its true and lasting meaning is not based on the beauty of the word.

I have taught in my workshops that we are one in the mind and body of God. I was totally unaware that people didn't know or understand that one-liner any more than they understood the word, oneness. It's not that people are stupid or that I'm a genius; it meant only they hadn't had my experiences and weren't able to fit the word into their modern-day concept of spiritual understanding.

Under karmic law and through religious teachings, we are taught there are two powers. I've already shared this countless times, but I needed to start somewhere to identify where the mass consciousness is. We have been taught, God is "outside" of us and that we are separate from Him, unless through His Grace, we become one of His "chosen."

On the spiritual path, as your awareness ascends above the

karmic law, you reach the place where you can see the violet Light. You begin to become aware, on a conscious level, everything is already one with God. It is not something you have to earn, but the reality of what already *is*.

When I taught that we are one in the mind of God and one in the body of Christ, I was offering a teaching that, in my opinion, said it all. In order to effectively teach you, however, how to use this information in your day-to-day life, please accept my apologies and see if these human words make that statement more understandable.

There is only *one mind*, (God's mind)—there is only *one body*, (the temple/body of God.) Though it appears there is you, me, and bazillions of other people in this world, there is still only one body. We appear to be separate and housed in bodies, but in spiritual reality, there is only one. We are individual expressions, manifesting outwardly as separate identities, but the truth is oneness.

Therefore, I'm not healing your body or mind, I'm healing my own. I can feel what you feel, so I place my hands on myself if you appear to be in another part of the world. Through my awareness that we are actually one, when I open my mind to the omnipresent (everywhere-present) source, the healing occurs.

If you are hurting long distance from me, and I can't physically reach on my own body where I'm feeling the pain, I would not be distressed. I would merely close my eyes, bring the violet Light to my awareness and the pain would then dissolve. Watch me carefully while I take this telephone call. After you see me in action, if you have any questions, I'll be sure to answer them.

The moment I hear a person on the end of the line say, "I need help" or "I'm hurting," I close my eyes immediately and silently say, Peace be with me. I am immediately and silently asking for the presence of God (which is the violet Light,) to fill my mind. I can listen to all they have to say and I will affirm, I am with you.

I will feel their fear. So will you, but the peace and presence is your armor so you are a neutral channel for that healing Light.

This woman shared that yesterday she awoke with a bladder infection. She made an appointment with a doctor. He insisted on giving her antibiotics. She explained that she can't take drugs because of serious reactions, however, the doctor has insisted that she must take them.

She trusted them and took the prescription medicine. She went to sleep last night with heart palpitations. This morning, she awoke, still having erratic heartbeats. She took the medicine, as requested throughout the day. She telephoned me just now, in great fear, because she just went to the bathroom the toilet was full of blood.

As I close my eyes and feel her pain, I can also feel a severe pain in her middle-lower back. I can't reach that area with my hand, on myself, nor on her across the miles. I feel her pain and allow the Light to dissolve that darkness within my own consciousness. Not hers. Mine. The pain dissolves and she gives me validation that the area no longer hurts her.

She's breathing shallowly, I know this because I, myself, can hardly take a deep breath. In that moment of helping another, trust what you are feeling is exactly what the person is feeling. I ask her to take a breath as deeply as she can, breathing in counting to seven, holding the breath, if possible, to the count of seven and exhaling to the count of seven.

As she is doing this, within my vision, I can see the darkness is beginning to lighten. Within my spiritual vision, I can still see only dark, heavy energy, so she and I must take another slow, deep breath. As we do this, I can feel myself getting the oxygen into my lungs. (If I am feeling this, so is she because we are truly one.) Fear restricts the breath. The breath is necessary for the channeling of the Light.

A third time, I ask her to take a slow, deep breath. I can see the darkness within dissolving, now the colors within are turning to a dirty yellow and green. The violet Light consumes these old buried emotions and the woman is sharing that she is feeling the warmth and love flowing through her entire body.

I place my right hand on my bladder, I can feel the excess heat (energy) within the woman. My hand is channeling the Light to rebalance that area and I can feel a cooling as the erratic energy is being balanced. The woman is healed and confirms there is no longer a burning sensation in her bladder.

Healing across the miles is this simple. I will check on her later tonight when I go into the Light to see if her body has assimilated all the energy I've filled her with. If so, I will send more to help her on her way to a complete recovery.

Listen to me carefully: Your first and automatic reaction to a person in need must be, "Peace be with me." After you have accomplished the first reaction, you can be human and fall apart if you want, right along with the person. But, your first reaction is the most important, to reach out to the Light, and make that contact.

Years ago, my sister, Vicki, was a registered nurse. She awakened me one morning, at approximately 5:00 A.M. Not being fully awake and looking at the time, I said, "Vicki, do you have any idea how early it is? Can't you call me back after the sun comes up?" Her voice, filled with fear responded, "No, I need you now."

Well, those words got my attention. I immediately closed my eyes and said, "Peace be with me." I asked her what was wrong.

As a nurse, that morning, she was giving an AIDS patient a shot. The syringe rolled over and punctured my sister's hand. She was immediately taken for tests and she was terrified, having been given all the new rules she and her husband would need to live by until the tests told her, months down the road, whether she had been infected.

My response to her was, "Vicki, I feel like you're going to be fine. I'll continue to work on this long distance, don't be scared, everything will be okay."

We talked for a while and hung up. It was early, but with the adrenaline rush, I was now fully awake. I headed down the hall to the kitchen to have coffee. In mid-stride, I stopped, dropped to my knees in fear and cried out, "My God. She could be infected with AIDS." I felt incredible fear, but by then, my human emotion would be dissolved in the Light that had already been called in. The tests run on Vicki were negative.

As humans, we continue to be mesmerized by the hypnotic suggestions of the human scene. I have taught men, women, and children how to do this. Each has successfully brought forth the violet

Light and consumed their pains, but then they think, "That was just coincidence it worked this time." They invalidate the power within themselves.

They doubt it will work again and won't continue to use it for each experience in their life. I get frustrated, because they won't use the information on a daily basis, but turn to me when they have the same ability. I can give you the awareness, but you must be the one to continue.

In each century, God has sent Lights into the world to keep His flame aglow. The information I'm sharing isn't new; it's been around forever. The Light will never cease to shine. If I lay down my life and can no longer be seen with human eyes, He will send another and another . . . until that day comes that each of His expressions finds their minds filled with the Light.

The world feels overwhelmed with insanity in various forms. We continue to look for the power to overcome it, praying to God to make the wars stop, to heal the sick, or to feed the multitudes. God has already given all that He is, He withholds nothing from us. The Light goes before us, acting through us, individually, giving and giving.

When there was a depression, there were no less fish in the sea or orchards filled with fruits. The only lack was in the people's awareness. There is no lack for anything that we, the human race, need and there never will be.

No superpower will erase the wars and insanity. The only power already exists within each of us, to open our minds to the ultimate place within ourselves and to allow it to manifest in and through us as our health, wealth, well being, desires, joy, and every other spiritual attribute that is our divine right. Not something you must earn by being a better human, but something you get by opening yourself to the true you *within*, allowing it to live through you.

It's not about retraining our minds by reading enough of the right books. It's about healing our minds, being led to the without, given our answers in a book because we're not trusting our own thoughts. As an author, with my love of writing, you would think I'd like to generate book sales, telling you that you need to read everything I ever write. It wouldn't be true. You can use my books (or another's, of course) as a tool for awareness, but once you have that awareness, then you must proceed accordingly.

What I'm teaching isn't hard. You ask for peace, and by closing your eyes to the outer world of appearances, you will enter a realm of golden silence. In a silent, holy moment, the contact is made and whether you feel a shift or electric shock, you will watch His glory made manifest.

You don't ask for houses, cars, money, healings on any level, or anything physical. God is spiritual, not physical. If you ask and receive His presence, everything will come to you. Seek ye first the Kingdom of Heaven and all else will be added. Heaven is a state of consciousness, an awareness, knowingness, an acceptance that your consciousness is God. Within that acknowledgment, all that He has ever given is yours.

When I would taste and smell purity, and people were healed, remember I would ask, "What in the hell is going on in my world?" His voice responded, "Before they call—I will answer."

He knows your needs before you do. The woman I healed on the telephone just now was thanking me. I said, "Thank God! He's the one who did it." Her response was, "I do thank God, but I thank you, too, Gloria, because you are the one who was and had to be plugged in for me to receive it."

For God's sake—for your sake—plug in. Turn to God for the sake of God and you will see miracles, one after another, manifesting in your world. If you are looking at "twoness," you have separated and disconnected yourself from the source. It's not my health or your health, it is God appearing *as* health.

It isn't my children and God's children, it is God appearing as children. It isn't my wealth and success, it's God appearing as wealth and success. It isn't my ideas and God's ideas, He expresses Himself through my individual mind.

Also, I haven't told you this, but as a healer, you have to drink lots of water. Water is a conductor of electricity, we all know that, right? I don't want you to rely on coffee or tea after you've performed a healing. Please drink at least one glass of water. As healers, we channel so much electricity, we will dehydrate ourselves if we're not careful.

Also, for your information, while you're working on people (or even afterward) you may find yourself burping or fluffying (passing gas). If that happens, it's just a part of the process of moving energy.

Fifteen years ago, when all these experiences began occurring, it was difficult for me to accept and understand. One morning, as I was sitting, drinking my early morning coffee, my attention was drawn to the sliding-glass doors in the dining room. They were covered with fingerprints from my two toddlers.

I quietly affirmed, "The power of God is within me, I want to use that power to clean that window." Nothing happened.

I looked up at the ceiling (looking beyond, to the heavens), and asked, "You're telling me I can heal the minds of mankind, being a little miracle worker, and I can't even take smudges off a window?" The inner, quiet, but bold voice within responded, "God doesn't do windows."

My first lesson was, God doesn't do effects, He is the first and one true cause. Second, I learned not to try to use God, but to allow Him to use me. Meaning, I no longer turned to Him begging or asking for anything of a physical nature. Instead, I ask, "How may I serve you?" My entire life changed when I figured that one out.

Oh, my goodness, I just looked at the clock. I must let you go home. I think you have plenty to think about for a while. I'd like you to think about all I've shared with you today, and if you come up with any questions, please write them down and I'll be sure to answer them.

I've certainly enjoyed this day with you. I will look forward to doing it again sometime. I'm going to ask for a heart-to-heart hug. I'd like you to rub your hands together before you place your arms around me, too. I want to feel cloaked in the arms of love, too. As we hug, close your eyes and watch for that pinpoint of white Light in the center of your vision.

Hug it, kiss it, bare it. Doesn't that heart-to-heart warmth feel better than anything you've ever felt in your life? God, I love you so much. Don't let go until I tell ya.

My prayer for you is this: May the peace and presence of God fill your mind and enfold you on this and every day of your life. I ask only that His grace gives you the spiritual vision to see your life and all life, in every person, place, and thing as He created it. From the Lord, God, our being, it is so!

Good night, be safe, be happy, you're in my heart and thoughts.

Always,
Gloria

Q: Does the violet Light look the same to everyone? Is it the same shape, shade, etc?

A: The violet Light flows in different patterns and appears as a kaleidoscope in my perspective. Sometimes it's a light lavender, sometimes a rich purple, and other times, tinged with rose. Most often for me, it's literally violet. I don't ever put any judgments on whatever color of that ray I'm seeing. I attempt to put more attention just on being at peace than what I'm visually experiencing.

Q: How do I get out of the muck I've created? I intellectually know that I need to get out of my own way, but I seem to be just spinning my wheels.

A: If I was in your shoes, the first thing I would do is recognize that I'm making a judgment about outer events, the perception that my life is filled with muck. I would immediately remember that I entertain only the divine in my consciousness, home, body, and experience. At the present, you are separating yourself from God, believing that you have a life separate and apart from that source. And because of that belief—it is true, by appearances.

Believing that it is "your" life and "His" life, you have now become dependent upon your human means to give you energy. Your energy is now limited. Your financial supply has become limited, also. Your opportunities are limited.

If you are looking at experiences such as these and feeling overwhelmed, you're not sure where to begin. To allow the changes in your life to occur, the first place you should begin is by surrendering every judgment and making it a point to open your mind for the Light the first chance on awakening and several times throughout the day.

By making contact and plugging into the source, you will be tapping back into the unlimited supply of energy and divine intelligence and you will soon find human perspectives melting away into nothingness.

You will find yourself no longer focusing on problems, but seeking only the presence of God, and in attaining that, your problems will be nonexistent.

Q: I've noticed that some people, while being healed, get sleepy, some are hot, and some are very cold. Why is that?
A: People do get extremely sleepy and the reason is twofold. First, if you have had a racing, busy mind your entire life and you are introduced to peace of mind for the first time, you have entered a new realm of consciousness. It's a state of consciousness where a person basks in bliss. Second, if a person has carried severe pain for a very long time, to have it immediately erased, leaves them feeling extremely tired. It takes a lot of energy to fight or carry pain.

Generally, for me, the people feel warmth from my hands (almost like they're built-in heating pads). There have been times for me, when the presence of God flows through me in waves of goosebumps. Whenever I feel goosebumps, I feel like God's talking to me, and whatever I'm hearing is the truth and I'd better darned well pay attention.

Overall, individuals will feel different. Either hot or cold is just an experience of energy flowing. Don't be absolute about either one, just accept that each experience is different.

Q: I see light around others, but I don't see colors when following the hands-on healing process. Will I still be effective?

A: If you are seeing light or colors around others with your eyes opened or closed, then I'm sure that you will eventually begin seeing the colors within your mind. If, after several minutes of laying-on-of-hands, you aren't seeing the colors—tip your head back, close your eyes, and "look within"—almost like you're looking out the top of your head. This will help lift the veil that separates the physical and spiritual world. If you still aren't seeing lights or colors within your vision, continue doing the hand positions, but be aware that the person perhaps truly doesn't want the healing, though he or she may say otherwise. Continue to channel the energy and be at peace.

Q: Why can I feel heat and cold in my hands, but not see the Light?

A. Your gift, at present, is more sensitive to the touch. With continued effort and practice, you will begin to see the Light. Years ago, long before I ever started having spiritual experiences, I had read a book called *The Reincarnation of Peter Proud.* I found the book fascinating. In it, Peter Proud spoke of dying and going through a tunnel of darkness and seeing the Light.

Every night, while going to sleep, I would imagine a white Light in the center of my inner vision and I would walk and walk and walk, trying to reach the light before falling asleep. I was unknowingly, at that time, expanding my awareness. For months, I would run, skip, and dance toward the Light, but as soon as I felt like I was getting close to it, it would be far off in the distance once again.

I persevered and continued to go to the Light. Years later, those practices paid off. Don't be afraid that it will take you years to see it or understand that you are already one with the Light. The acceptance can occur in the twinkling of an eye.

Q: Why don't I see a violet Light? I see green or blue-green.

A: When you see a green Light, it is telling you that healing and harmony within the consciousness/body is occurring. A blue-green Light would tell you that the spiritual body is being worked on and that it will manifest in the physical body. If you aren't yet seeing the violet Light, continue asking for the peace and presence of God. Doing so quickens the expanding of consciousness. The violet Light is the Christ consciousness that is *within* you and everyone, ever awaiting you, as you open fully to it.

Q: Why do we need to balance the physical with the spiritual?

A: Please, read this book again and again, until that would never be a concern. The spiritual world is a state of consciousness that God created, the spiritual reality held within His mind concerning each individual expression of Himself. When you tap into that realm of consciousness, that one life that He has created begins expressing itself in your physical world. That world that begins appearing without you taking thought for your home, health, food, companionship, etc. It is the return to Eden where only one power, one presence, one experience exists and is maintained and can never be humanly defiled.

The physical world, at present, is filled with appearances of insanity, sadness, lack, pain, heartache, confusion, and fear in various disguises. When the physical is balanced with the spiritual, all those appearances fade from sight and only the good that stands behind the appearance shines through. Humans will still enjoy the senses of being a human, without the insanity. Balance of the physical and spiritual world brings the greatest and truest form of joy and a peace that passeth all human understanding.

Q: Do I have to concentrate on the people I'm doing absentee healing on?

A: No, in fact, you would never take a name or even a claim of disease into the Light. All you would ask for is the peace and presence of God and when you have that your individual mind will be flooded with Light, erasing the human error and misperception of the original request for healing. Once that belief is dissolved in the Light, the miracle will occur in your outer world.

Q: How do I deal with feeling so silly and stupid when I find out that healing and plugging into spirit is so simple after spend-

ing great amounts of time and money seeking through more difficult methods, involving ritual?

A: Evolving from a human being to a spiritual being can never be considered stupid, no matter what form or steps you have taken to become more aware. Once when I was standing before a large group, I opened my speech with the following: "Ladies and Gentlemen, I come before you, to stand behind you, to tell you something which I know nothing about. Next Thursday, which is Good Friday, there will be a men's meeting that only ladies can attend. Admission is free, pay at the door, sit on the floor, and we'll discuss the four corners of the round table. With all of the fast talkers, double talkers, and smooth talkers out there is there any reason *why* we're so confused?"

False beliefs and fear have been ingrained in the mass consciousness for countless eons. To be part of an era of souls awakening to the truth is a great honor, one that your soul chose at this moment of eternity. Whatever methods people have chosen to awaken must be looked upon without judgment. We're all doing the best we can, at every given moment, with the awareness that we have.

To have spent large sums of money on tools or awareness can never be looked upon as stupid. Souls, in this golden age, are hungry for the truth and will continue to seek until they feel they have found the answers. Even after you have plugged in direct to spirit and get your answers and energy direct, the growing continues. Biblical teachings state, "These and greater things you will also do." He fulfills all promises.

Enjoy the journey and if you find yourself enjoying ritual, then heal the judgment that it's bad and enjoy the tools and ceremony. They, too, are here for your growth.

Q: Sometimes ego gets in my way. How do I move it aside?

A: First of all, unless we're talking about two different things, it's my belief that ego isn't bad. "Ego" means conscious mind. It is necessary to have an individual expression and personality. Within the ego is where the gift of discernment lives. We are never asked to give up our ego because it is an expression of ourselves. Your mind is an avenue of awareness through which the thoughts and inspiration of God flow.

It doesn't need to be difficult to quiet the mind. While you are lying or sitting, you request that peace fill your mind. Your mind will wander, of course, and do other things. As soon as you become aware that the mind is wandering, don't judge it as bad, thinking you can't meditate. Instead, give the mind permission to wander, but as soon as you become aware that it is wandering, gently ask again, Peace be with me.

I find myself wandering and probably always will, but I don't beat myself up or tell myself that it's wrong. It enables me to develop a deeper and longer concentration on the Light.

Q: Do you believe that healing occurs on many levels—physical, emotional mental, and spiritual?

A: Yes, not only on those levels, but morally, financially, and politically. On all levels. Each of us who is able to tap into the source and bring that Light to this dimension is doing far more than we are aware. The master is a mediator, bringing that spiritual Light to those who have not yet expanded their awareness. It's what He has done for me. My greatest service now is not in being an author or mother, an executive secretary, accountant, or any other profession, but being a mediator. I am a channel to bring the spiritual Light to others who have not, as yet, reached that state of awareness.

When you plug in direct, you also become a mediator and you will witness the healing of your mind affecting everyone around you. You can't carry the Light without others around you noticing and being affected, also.

Q: Do you ever try to send a specific color when you focus healing for people?

A: I only see the red/orange/yellow/green/blue/or pink as I'm doing an overhaul on someone. Though the colors may be pretty and come together in a kaleidoscope pattern, I don't attempt to call them forth. The violet Light is the only color that I will reach out for or open myself to because it is what heals on all levels. I have never read books about color therapy, so I'm not an authority by any means of what they may accomplish. For me, personally, I only depend upon the activity of Christ (which is the violet Light).

Q: How can I bring my mind to peace when I feel fear for someone I'm attempting to heal, especially a child?

A: The only thing I can say about this is that for some reason, when I close my eyes, and I can't physically see the problem, my mind quiets without human effort. There are times that I must chant, "Peace, peace, peace be with me," but those times are rare.

I'm not asking people to stick their heads in the sand and ignore possible dangerous or life-threatening situations. If someone is bleeding severely, you should call 911 or drive them to a hospital emergency room. If someone else was available to do the driving, of course, you could lay hands on the person and close your eyes, asking for peace.

My mother called me several years ago, telling me that she was having trouble breathing and asked me what she should do. I responded, "You should get your butt in the car and go to the emergency room now." I shared that I would go into the Light immediately and send healing energy as she was on her way for medical help.

I heard from my mom following this and she said that by the time she got to the hospital, she could breathe, but that had the tests run anyway. The results came back that everything was normal. I would never tell someone not to go to a doctor. Until our awareness is raised to the degree that we can meet every situation, we must depend upon other methods, also. Surrender guilt if you believe that it's wrong to continue using doctors. They are here in service to us.

Even if you close your eyes, you may still feel fear—but it is the other person's fear that you are feeling. If your state of mind is peaceful, the person will begin feeling it as their fear begins to dissolve. Practice, you'll see.

Q: What's the best way to release your (own) feelings of lack of self-worth or of not being good enough?

A: From my own experiences, I couldn't understand why God would ask me to awaken His children. I was a nice person, but I also had some shadows and I'd been taught that I'd have to be perfect before I could ever know Him. In the Bible it says, "Only those who are pure of heart will ever see God." Well, I definitely wasn't pure of heart (in my opinion), and yet I had seen Him on countless occasions.

The definition of "pure of heart" sounds mighty boring to those in this physical world: no eating meat, drinking, smoking, cussing, lusting after another, etc. I don't know anyone, including me, who doesn't do some or all of the above. However, from a spiritual sense, being pure in heart means loving others for the sake of loving them, without wondering, What's in it for me? My intent is pure. I offer to give and give, never thinking about what I might get out of it.

My mom used to say, "You give to a fault, Gloria." My greatest pleasure comes from giving.

You must begin healing the child within. Where do you feel the lack of self-worth coming from? Who told you that you're not good enough? God once asked me, "Who told you that I would hurt you? And who told you that you're bad? These are untruths!"

It's sometimes easier to believe all the bad things that others tell us than to believe the good. Begin saying ten nice things about yourself every time you start to focus on one of your weaknesses, and remember, something that you may perceive about yourself as a weakness, with a new perspective, could actually be a spiritual strength. Surrender the judgment concerning yourself and allow Him to manifest the truth.

Q: What's the most important thing I need to know?

A: Eight simple words that a lifer in prison said: "If you've got God, you've got it all!" If you have the presence of God you won't know lack, hunger, disease, anger, hatred, or fear. You will finally and completely truly know yourself.

Q: When does the soul come into the body?

A: Approximately nine years ago, I asked myself the same question. Others around me were talking about abortion issues. I could never share an opinion, because I didn't know enough about pro or con to answer or give an opinion. In silence one evening, I asked, and the response followed that the soul doesn't actually enter until approximately two-to-four weeks before delivery. The consciousness begins melding with the mother at approximately six to seven months.

I was told that the baby "knows" beforehand if the mother is going to abort and doesn't enter. Also, crib death occurs because a soul has entered, but then feels like it's not able to withstand the lessons in this life and departs. God gives us life, He doesn't take it away. God is life.

These are inspirational messages that have been shared with me and I'm now sharing with you. The awareness has brought me comfort on more than one occasion. Personally, I don't feel that I would ever have been able to abort, wanting to have children the way I did, but I don't hold judgment toward those who have made that decision.

Q: How will I ever attain the confidence to heal other people like you?

A: My confidence never came from the personality level because I know that it's not me who's doing the healings. A human cannot build confidence; it manifests as a result of witnessing the miraculous events that begin to appear. Begin by healing your own life and those who are closest to you, which can be done without saying a word. Practicing silently, in the beginning, will alleviate a fear of failing.

Practice feeling for the hot and cold spots and nurture your family and loved ones on a silent level and, as you begin to feel more confident, you will then openly be able to help others.

Q: You've said that you accept donations through your Miracle Healing Ministry, but that you don't charge for healing people. Am I wrong to charge people for my time and services?

A: This question has been brought to my attention for years and I can only ask you a question in response, Why are you becoming a healer? What are you in it for? Are you doing it for attention, to be admired, to receive gratitude, fame, or fortune? If you get nothing out of it at all, except love as the payment, are you okay with that? If you are loving people unconditionally, above and beyond their outer personality and even if you don't like them, you can still heal them as if they were Christ, Himself, then you are a true healer. If you're loving for the sake of loving (the only reason to be of service), remembering that those who deserve it the least, are the ones who need it the most, then you will be paid in endless forms.

I've shared with people, also, that if they put a $60 pricetag on an hour of healing work, they have just limited their return. Some people won't donate, but others will give more than you ever thought possible. In either case, it's God inspiring the giving and the presence will always make sure that you have everything you need.

If you charge out of fear or believing it is your supply, you will have blocked your flow, not only in getting, but in receiving. Give from the heart and if you don't feel like doing it, even though an appointment is made, don't follow through with it. If you're not giving totally and completely, you're not helping anyone.

Q: You speak of not being able to keep a secret. Does this mean that if I wanted to open up to you and share my most awful moments and experiences (that I feel shame over) that you would blab it to the world?

A: No. I'm the friendly neighborhood priest and I would honor your secrets and shame and would never tell another soul. My point in saying that I can't keep a secret is to tell you that there are no secrets and a moment is coming in everyone's life when there will be nothing left to hide.

If you have experiences that you're feeling shame over, they are the first memories that I would suggest be healed. You are holding guilt and condemnation for yourself and will attract others to judge you, because you are judging yourself as being bad for doing whatever it is that you have done. When you surrender those judgments against yourself, the healing will occur and you will also be able to make your life an open book and will ultimately give others a safe place to expose their true selves.

Q: You mention that when a person feels fear or wants to plug into the source they should close their eyes and see a pin-point of white Light in the center of their vision. What does the pinpoint of white Light mean?
A: When you see a flicker of Light (almost like a Christmas tree light) in the center of your vision, your individual mind has opened in order for the violet Light to begin flowing.

Q: What does it mean if I see white Lights in other places within my inner vision?
A: Spirit has told me that a bright white Light at the extreme left of your vision is your Christ Light/Higher Power. If you see pinpoints of white Light at the upper left of your vision, those are angels. If you see bright white Lights to the upper right of your vision, those are spiritual guides. When you see random pinpoints of white Light, these are souls from the other side of the veil or in the physical realm, reaching out to touch your healing state of consciousness.

Q: Is it imperative that we feel the other person's pain and symptoms when we work on them, in order for them to get healed? It seems like you said that if you don't feel the pain, you can't heal it.
A: It is not imperative for you to feel another person's pain, because as you are channeling the pure energy to them, it is divine intelligence and knows where to go and what to do. The reason I feel what another feels is because it is one of my guiding forces to tell me where next to place my hands. As soon as I place my hands on their pain, the Light dissolves the pain in me, and when I no longer can feel it, neither can the person and I have immediate validation that they are healed.

Q: How do you develop the ability to feel the other person's pain and symptoms if we are, as yet, unable to do so?

A: The ability to feel another's pain is called clairsentience/empathy, and it's a spiritual gift that we all are given. Some use it and others numb it, because to feel what everyone around you is feeling can be overwhelming to some. If you are to be a healer for many people, the gift will surface and it will serve you. You will also become more intuitive and, through that knowingness, you will be able to discern what is your pain or another's. There will be no confusion as you continue allowing the Light to use you as an instrument to heal. It's all a part of the growing and accepting process.

Q: How do you develop the X-ray vision if you don't have it? What is a good way to practice it and also, do you see with your mind's eye or do you see with your physical eyes behind your closed eyelids with the back of the lids being the screen?

A: I like to call the scanning within a body, imagination. If you think what you're seeing is just your imagination, then it won't matter if you're right or wrong, because it's just a game. You could sit in a church or mall or anywhere in public and look at people for a few minutes, close your eyes and see the different colors within their energy field. You could also have a group of friends over and practice on one another.

I'm not able to see with my physical eyes, except on rare occasions. I view a person for a few seconds, close my eyes, and use my mind's eye. Some people, however, can see the energy fields with their eyes open.

Q: How do you develop the ability to have the ringing of the ears?

A: To me, that's a funny question, because most people I meet ask if I am able to heal their ears so they *don't* ring. To receive the tones, however, is the gift of clairaudience, and placing your hands over your ears daily will keep that spiritual center open and activated.

Q: Can *everyone* develop the gifts of clairvoyance, clairaudience, clairsentience, etc? If you've never done this or had the
ability to do these things up until now, is it still possible to
miraculously be able to develop them later in life?

A: Everyone, within themselves, is spiritually gifted with all of
these talents. For most, they lay dormant until each soul begins to
spiritually awaken to them. Remember that even modern science
tells us that we only use a small fraction of our mind. It doesn't
matter what age you are, you can learn to tap into your true nature.
(I've taught the elderly how to do this and they were extremely
jazzed.)

Q: Is everyone supposed to feel the electric shocks and shifts,
which tell us that the other person is healed? How can you develop the abilities to do so if you don't experience them yet?
Please describe the ways they can feel.

A: Everyone *has* felt the electric shocks, to some degree. Some
nights, when you're falling asleep and all of a sudden, you jerk
wildly, this is a form of the electric shocks I'm talking about. Most
people think that their muscles are relaxing, but in reality, for a
millisecond they were between the conscious and superconscious
levels and plugging into the source. The electric shocks occur in
the silence, just milliseconds before you would enter dream time.

The shifts can feel like energy moving beneath your hands, little pops under their skin (or yours, since you feel what they do),
and sometimes they are on such a subtle level that you may even
think that you or the other person has gas. A small, unexpected
twitch is another form of a shift, and each of these is telling you
that a blocked energy has opened within and the electricity is now
flowing again.

Q: How does it work that people who are merely in the same
room with you can be healed without you ever even working on
them and then not even knowing what's going on? Will we all
get to do that?

A: Practice with a friend. Sit in the same room but position yourselves so that you can not see each other's hands. Lay your hand on the right knee and ask your friend to tell you where your hand is. Practice feeling and dissolving each other's pain. You will receive validation.

The Light I carry at that moment will affect those who enter my consciousness/home/experience. If I have plugged in direct to the source, they will feel an automatic peaceful, serene sense about me, which they will assume.

Yes, as you heighten your state of consciousness, others around you will experience the pure love that will emanate from your presence.

Q: Has anyone you have taught so far been able to do healings of the magnitude and miracles that you do?

A: First of all, there is no order of difficulty in miracle working. Each miracle is a manifestation of love. I am not teaching people how to perform miracles, for that is an effect. My purpose is to teach how to be one with the first and only true cause, that power that is the real you.

If I have given the wrong impression that it is miracles we are seeking, then I have failed in my teachings, for seeking effects would only be more human gratification for the senses. You seek God for the sake of God, and if, in the course of events, miracles manifest moment to moment, then you are, indeed, blessed.

In answer to your question, however, yes. Others have put this awareness to practice, even those at the age of eight or ten and have proven that what I teach and live is demonstrated.

Q: Do you always place your hands on your heart center when you do absentee healings?

A: No. If a person has called me concerning an earache in their left ear, I would rub my hands and place them on my left ear. In the beginning stages, you will place your hand wherever a pain within you or another is, but as you continue to invite the presence of God into your life, you won't have to actually lay hands on. It is a person's mind that is being healed, the body is the effect. Most people feel like you're providing a service by laying hands on the

body, but the healing is actually occurring within the consciousness and then manifesting outwardly in the body.

**Q: If you happen to hear of someone through the TV news
or newspaper who has been seriously injured or ill, can you automatically send them a healing, or do you have to get their permission or have them ask you for a healing?**

A: I used to ask, at the soul level, if it was appropriate to do a
healing and, in ten years, I was only guided to back off once. In
that situation, the person requesting a healing was also a healer
(for the masses) and she needed to accept her healing powers for
her own need. Every other request was accepted by spirit.

When the Oklahoma City bombing occurred, I sent Light to
the situation. If I had had the finances to go, I would have physically gone. I have sent healings to many wealthy people as well as
to poor people as I'm driving through their neighborhoods.

The healings are the purest love there is. A person of any race
or creed can accept at the soul level or not. The healing will appear outwardly when the person is ready to accept it. Give all healings in the name of love and don't wait for the effect, but know
that through your pure intent it has been given and released unconditionally. Be at peace.

**Q: How do you heal yourself if you find yourself ill? What
hand positions do you use for self?**

A: All of the hand positions you have learned here, except for
the figure-eight down the spine, can be done on yourself. If you are
hurting, rub your hands and place them at the point of pain, close
your eyes, and allow the violet Light to fill your mind.

**Q: What did you mean when you said that 5 percent of the
masses has the ability to heal the multitudes and that the rest of
humanity has the ability to heal themselves? How would I know
if I'm one of the 5 percent?**

A. Five percent of the masses are healers. Not everyone wants
to heal the multitudes, for they have their own talents of song-
writing, singing, inventing, accounting, etc. Everyone can heal

their life, but not everyone is going to choose to do so. You would know if you're one of the 5 percent of healers who can heal multitudes of people if that is your individual calling. Do you love people so much, sometimes, that it physically hurts? Are there times when you're filled with so much love that if you don't give it away to someone, you have to walk on the grass, hug a tree or kiss a rock? If you have that much love for humanity flowing through you, then I would say that you are definitely in the 5 percent.

Q: I notice that Jesus works very closely with you. Will He also be working closely with everyone who does this work or is it that He happens to be working with you because He is your master teacher. Do you have a past-life connection with Him?

A: Not everyone would accept Him and for those who do not, other ascended masters appear. Yes, He is my master teacher, and yes, I do have a past-life connection to Him. I know the first time He came to me, in 1981, that it wasn't the first time I ever had seen Him.

If you choose to have Him as a master teacher, you can call out to Him and He will be there for you.

Q: Are people who have had a Oneness Ceremony or experiences similar to it more connected or plugged in to the source and healing power than people who haven't had an experience like that?

A: This question is exactly why I don't usually mention that experience. I don't want people hung up on the idea that if they don't have such a ceremony that they can't do as I do. The experience was wonderful, of course, but it, too, is an effect of God. Remember, I said that I want you to seek God for the sake of God—and then as abundance, joy, or spiritual experiences begin to appear in your life, that's all well and good. But, you're not originally going to God so that those things will happen. (Well, some of you probably are, but if you do, you're going to block the true experiences from ever occurring.)

I don't really want to play down the experience, but I feel like I need to so that you aren't putting so much emphasis on it. My

Oneness Ceremony was something that I needed. Otherwise, I might not have ever accepted everything else that was going to begin following and I might not have been able to do it at the level at which I do, publicly.

You must accept your current level of awareness and that each time you open to that violet Light, your awareness will be heightened. God only knows when that moment will come when you have a conscious awareness of your oneness with Him.

I believe that everyone will have a divine experience and that when it occurs, whether in this life or another, truly doesn't matter. All that matters is now.

During the past sixteen years, Gloria has taught people of all ages how to close their eyes and open their minds to unlimited, pure love (which restores the soul and physical world.)

Gloria holds out her hands to you, not to take from you, but to offer you her loving support.

OTHER WRITINGS AVAILABLE BY GLORIA D. BENISH

As God Is My Witness
ISBN 0-9636100-0-7 ($9.95*)

This book wrote itself through Gloria in eighteen hours. Spirit has used this book as a tool to take you on a gentle journey, through a mock trial, to heal fear, guilt, and judgment. Recapture a memory of your innocence as this divine message touches your heart.

To Become as Little Children
(Fairy tales for adults for the child in you . . .)
ISBN 0-9636100-1-5 ($16.95*)

Forty-five fairy tales for adults, all based on true experiences, dreams, revelations, and modern-day miracles. Inspirational, self-help/recovery for adult children, all written with happily-ever-after new beginnings. (Ten color illustrations by Linda K. Fudge.)

*Available at bookstores or visit www.miraclehealing.org

ABOUT THE AUTHOR

Gloria D. Benish was born October 5, 1953, in Pierre, South Dakota, the middle child of five children. In 1985, she heard the voice of spirit speak aloud, requesting her to "write a book that will awaken millions and millions of My children from their past slumber of negative beliefs and fears, as well as healing the minds of mankind."

Miracles began occurring through her, sometimes with a slight touch and oftentimes with no touch at all. The writings began immediately. Never searching for a word or phrase, Gloria wrote the books by listening to what was being dictated. She has written fourteen books, all based on true, modern-day miracles.

As a housewife and mother to four children, Gloria demonstrates how to live a life in a physical spiritual world. She teaches children, as well as adults, how to heal their lives.